Trauma Bonding

A guide to breaking free and healing from an abusive relationship

Harper Emerson

Contents

Copyrights	IV
1. An Introduction to Trauma Bonding	1
2. Understanding Trauma Bonding	5
3. Types of Trauma Bonding	9
4. Identifying Trauma Bonds	19
5. Breaking the Chains	35
6. Rebuilding and Healing	47
7. Preventing Future Bonds	59
8. Recap of Key Concepts	71
9. Life After Trauma Bonding	75
10. More Information on Trauma Bonding	81
About the Author	85
Also By	87
Other books written by Harper Emerson	

Copyright © 2024 by Harper Emerson

All rights reserved.

No portion of this book may be reproduced in any form without written permission from the publisher or author, except as permitted by U.S. copyright law.

This publication is designed to provide accurate and authoritative information in regard to the subject matter covered. It is sold with the understanding that neither the author nor the publisher is engaged in rendering legal, investment, accounting or other professional services. While the publisher and author have used their best efforts in preparing this book, they make no representations or warranties with respect to the accuracy or completeness of the contents of this book and specifically disclaim any implied warranties of merchantability or fitness for a particular purpose. No warranty may be created or extended by sales representatives or written sales materials. The advice and strategies contained herein may not be suitable for your situation. You should consult with a professional when appropriate. Neither the publisher nor the author shall be liable for any loss of profit or any other commercial damages, including but not limited to special, incidental, consequential, personal, or other damages.

Chapter One

An Introduction to Trauma Bonding

1.1: Definition of Trauma Bonding:

The term "trauma bonding" refers to a multifaceted psychological phenomenon in which an individual develops a strong emotional connection or attachment to someone who is harmful, abusive, or manipulative. This bond typically forms in situations where there is a power imbalance, and the victim experiences intermittent reinforcement of reward and punishment. Despite the harmful nature of the relationship, the victim becomes emotionally attached to the abuser, making it difficult for them to break free. This bond is often rooted in a cycle of abuse, apology, and affection, creating a sense of dependency and conflicting emotions within the victim. Trauma bonding can occur in various relationships, such as intimate partner relationships, familial connections, or within cults and other manipulative groups.

1.2: Significance and Impact on Mental Health

The term "trauma bonding" refers to a multifaceted psychological phenomenon in which an individual develops a strong emotional connection or attachment to someone who is harmful, abusive, or manipulative. This bond typically forms in situations where there is a power imbalance, and the victim experiences intermittent reinforcement of reward and punishment. Despite the harmful nature of the relationship, the victim becomes emotionally attached to the abuser, making it difficult for them to break free. This bond is often rooted in a cycle of abuse, apology, and affection, creating a sense of dependency and conflicting emotions within the victim. Trauma bonding can occur in various relationships, such as intimate partner relationships, familial connections, or within cults and other manipulative groups.

Emotional Turmoil: Individuals in trauma bonds often experience conflicting emotions. They may feel love, fear, and loyalty toward the abuser, creating a significant emotional turmoil.

Cognitive Distortions: Trauma bonding can lead to distorted perceptions of reality, making it challenging for the person to recognize the abusive nature of the relationship. This distortion can contribute to self-blame and a sense of unworthiness.

Self Esteem and Identity Issues: Continuous exposure to abuse and manipulation can lead to a gradual erosion of self-esteem. The victim may start to internalize negative messages from the abuser, resulting in diminished self-worth.

Identity Crisis: Trauma bonding can contribute to an identity crisis as the victim may become entangled in the abuser's narrative and lose a sense of their own identity and values.

Isolation from Support Systems: Victims of trauma bonding may withdraw from family and friends due to shame, fear, or the abuser's influence. This isolation can exacerbate feelings of loneliness and helplessness.

Physical Health Impacts: The chronic stress associated with trauma bonding can contribute to various physical health problems, including headaches, gastrointestinal issues, and a weakened immune system.

Repetition of Unhealthy Patterns: Individuals who have experienced trauma bonding may unintentionally seek out or recreate similar unhealthy patterns in future relationships, perpetuating a cycle of abuse.

Difficulty Establishing Healthy Boundaries: Bonding can make it challenging for individuals to establish and maintain healthy boundaries in relationships. This difficulty may further contribute to the perpetuation of abuse.

Post-Traumatic Stress Disorder (PTSD): Prolonged exposure to traumatic situations within a trauma bond can lead to the development of PTSD, characterized by intrusive thoughts, flashbacks, hypervigilance, and emotional numbing.

Impact on Decision Making: Trauma bonding can impair an individual's ability to make rational decisions, as emotions and dependency on the abuser may override logical thinking.

Barriers to Seeking Help: Victims may fear abandonment or retaliation from the abuser if they attempt to seek help or leave the relationship, creating additional barriers to reaching out for support. Understanding these impacts is crucial for developing effective interventions and support systems to help individuals break free from trauma bonds and rebuild their mental health. Professional therapeutic interventions and a supportive community can play a vital role in this process. The purpose of this book is to provide a comprehensive and empathetic resource for individuals who are grappling with trauma bonding, as well as for professionals and support networks aiming to assist those affected. The book seeks to shed light on the intricate dynamics of trauma bonding, offering insights into its psychological underpinnings, the various contexts in which it manifests, and, most importantly, practical strategies for breaking free from its grip. By addressing the complexities of trauma bonding, the book aims to empower readers with knowledge and tools to navigate their way out of abusive or harmful relationships. The primary purpose is to foster self-awareness, resilience, and a sense of agency, ultimately promoting healing and recovery. The book encompasses a broad range of aspects related to trauma bonding, providing a holistic understanding and guidance for individuals at various stages of their experiences.

The key components of the book include:

In Depth Understanding: The book delves into the psychological mechanisms that contribute to the formation and perpetuation of trauma bonds. It explores the impact of trauma on the brain and emotions, helping readers comprehend the root causes of their emotional entanglements.

Recognition and Identification: The book offers insights into recognizing the signs and symptoms of trauma bonding, facilitating self-reflection and aiding individuals in identifying whether they are in such a relationship.

Real Life Examples: Through case studies and real-life examples, the book illustrates diverse scenarios of trauma bonding, making the content relatable and providing readers with different perspectives that resonate with their experiences.

Practical Strategies for Breaking Free: The book provides practical advice and actionable strategies for breaking the chains of trauma bonding. This includes guidance on seeking professional help, building a support network, and developing coping mechanisms. (You may wish to consider purchasing the companion workbook

Rebuilding and Empowerment: We explore the process of rebuilding one's life after trauma bonding. It covers topics such as establishing healthy boundaries, self-care practices, and fostering personal growth and empowerment.

Preventative Measures: The book addresses preventative measures by promoting education and awareness. It aims to equip readers with the knowledge to recognize potential red flags in relationships and foster resilience to prevent future instances of trauma bonding.

Chapter Two

Understanding Trauma Bonding

2:1: The Psychology Behind Trauma Bonding Definition of Trauma:

Trauma is a psychological and emotional response to an event or series of events that are distressing or disturbing, often involving a sense of threat, harm, or danger. Traumatic experiences can overwhelm an individual's ability to cope and may leave lasting effects on their mental, emotional, and physical well-being. Trauma can result from a wide range of events, including but not limited to accidents, natural disasters, violence, abuse, loss, or witnessing distressing incidents. It is important to note that individuals may perceive and react to events differently, and what constitutes trauma can vary from person to person. The impact of trauma can manifest in various ways, influencing thoughts, emotions, behavior, and interpersonal relationships. Additionally, trauma can contribute to the development of mental health conditions such as post-traumatic stress disorder (PTSD).

How Trauma Bonds Form:

Trauma bonds form through a complex interplay of psychological, emotional, and biological factors. These bonds are typically established in situations where an individual experiences a combination of intermittent reward and punishment within a relationship. Here's a breakdown of the key elements in the formation of trauma bonds:

Intermittent Reinforcement:

Trauma bonds often develop in environments where the abuser provides intermittent positive reinforcement. This could be in the form of affection, apologies, or brief periods of kindness. These intermittent rewards create a sense of hope and attachment, even amid abusive or harmful behavior.

Power Imbalance:
Trauma bonds are more likely to form in relationships characterized by a significant power imbalance. This could be in intimate partner relationships, familial connections, or within manipulative groups. The power dynamic contributes to a sense of dependency on the more dominant or controlling individual.

Isolation and Dependence:
The abuser often isolates the victim, cutting them off from external support systems. This isolation increases the victim's dependence on the abuser for emotional and sometimes even physical needs. The lack of external perspectives reinforces the distorted view of the relationship.

Manipulation and Gaslighting:
Manipulative tactics, such as gaslighting (psychological manipulation to make the victim doubt their own perceptions or sanity), contribute to the confusion and self-doubt experienced by the victim. This manipulation can distort the victim's reality and make it difficult for them to recognize the abusive nature of the relationship.

Traumatic Bonding in Adversity:
Shared experiences of adversity, such as going through difficult times together, can create a sense of connection and bonding. In situations where the abuser alternates between causing distress and providing comfort, the victim may form a bond as a coping mechanism.

Psychological Survival Mechanism:
Trauma bonds can be seen as a psychological survival mechanism. The victim may develop a strong emotional attachment to the abuser to cope with the stress and uncertainty of the relationship. The bond serves as a survival strategy to maintain a connection in the hope of avoiding further harm.

Childhood Attachment Patterns:
Early childhood experiences with caregivers can influence the formation of trauma bonds later in life. Individuals with insecure attachment styles may be more susceptible to developing bonds with abusive individuals, seeking the familiar even if it is harmful.

Biological Factors:
Neurobiological processes play a role in trauma bonding. The brain may release bonding hormones, such as oxytocin, during moments of positive reinforcement, creating a physiological attachment to the abuser. Understanding how trauma bonds form is crucial for interventions aimed at breaking free from these patterns. Breaking the cycle often involves a combination of self-awareness, professional therapy, and support from a network of understanding and empathetic individuals.

2.2: Neurobiological Aspects

Neurobiological aspects play a crucial role in the formation and maintenance of trauma bonds. The brain's response to stress and attachment dynamics is complex, involving various neurotransmitters and hormonal systems. Here are some key neurobiological aspects related to trauma bonding:

Oxytocin and Bonding:
Oxytocin, often referred to as the "bonding hormone" or "love hormone," is released in the brain during positive social interactions, including moments of affection and connection. In abusive relationships, even if these moments are intermittent, the release of oxytocin can contribute to the formation of emotional bonds.

Dopamine and Reward Pathways:
Dopamine is a neurotransmitter associated with pleasure and reward. The intermittent reinforcement of positive behaviors by the abuser can stimulate the brain's reward pathways, creating a craving for the positive experiences and reinforcing the bond.

Stress Response and Cortisol:
Traumatic experiences activate the body's stress response, leading to the release of cortisol. Chronic exposure to stress and elevated cortisol levels can impact the hippocampus, a brain region involved in memory and emotional regulation. This may contribute to the persistence of trauma related memories and emotional reactions.

Amygdala Activation:
The amygdala, a part of the brain involved in processing emotions, particularly fear and pleasure, can become hyperactive in response to trauma. This heightened activation may enhance the emotional significance of the abuser, reinforcing the bond.

Chapter Three

Types of Trauma Bonding

3:1: Intimate Partner Violence:

Intimate Partner Violence (IPV), also known as domestic violence or relationship abuse, refers to a pattern of abusive behavior within an intimate relationship that is used by one partner to gain and maintain power and control over the other. This type of violence can occur in heterosexual or same sex relationships and can affect individuals of any age, race, ethnicity, socioeconomic status, or educational background.

Key aspects of Intimate Partner Violence include:

Physical Abuse:
The use of force that causes bodily harm, injury, or impairment. This includes hitting, slapping, punching, kicking, or any form of physical aggression.

Emotional or Psychological Abuse:
Controlling behaviors, verbal abuse, threats, intimidation, humiliation, and isolation that undermine the victim's self-worth and autonomy.

Sexual Abuse:
Coercing or forcing the partner into sexual acts without consent, including rape or any form of sexual assault.

Financial Abuse:
Controlling or restricting the victim's access to financial resources, employment, or economic independence.

The Cycle of Violence:
IPV often follows a cyclic pattern that includes a tension building phase, an acute or violent phase, and a reconciliation or honeymoon phase. The cyclical nature can make it challenging for victims to leave the abusive relationship.

Risk Factors:
Certain factors may increase the risk of IPV, including a history of violence or abuse, substance abuse, mental health issues, and societal factors such as gender inequality and cultural norms that condone or overlook violence.

Impact on Victims Physical Consequences:
Injuries, chronic health problems, or even death as a result of physical abuse

Emotional and Psychological Impact:
Anxiety, depression, low self-esteem, post-traumatic stress disorder (PTSD), and suicidal thoughts.

Social Consequences:
Isolation from friends and family, difficulty maintaining employment, and challenges in forming and maintaining healthy relationships.

Barriers to Leaving:
Victims of IPV often face significant barriers to leaving the abusive relationship, such as fear of retaliation, financial dependence, social isolation, and psychological manipulation.

Legal Consequences:
IPV is a violation of the law in many jurisdictions. Legal consequences can include restraining orders, criminal charges, and penalties for the perpetrator.

Children and IPV:
Children in households where IPV occurs may witness the abuse, leading to emotional and behavioral problems. They may also become direct targets of abuse.

Prevention and Intervention:
Prevention and intervention efforts include community education, awareness campaigns, legal protections, shelters for victims, and counseling services. Encouraging a culture of respect, equality, and open communication is crucial. It's important for individuals experiencing IPV to seek help and support. Various organizations, hotlines, and resources are available to assist victims in leaving abusive situations and starting the journey toward healing and safety.

3.2: Impact on Children Living with Parents in a Trauma Bond Relationship:
Living with parents in a trauma bond relationship can have profound and lasting effects on children. A trauma bond is characterized by the intense emotional connection between individuals who have experienced shared traumatic events, often resulting in unhealthy dynamics. Here's a detailed exploration of the impact on children in such an environment:

Emotional Instability:
Observation of Conflict:
Children in a household with trauma bonded parents witness frequent conflicts and emotional volatility. The unpredictable nature of these conflicts can lead to heightened anxiety and a constant state of emotional instability.

Attachment Issues:
Insecure Attachments:
Children may develop insecure attachment styles due to inconsistent caregiving and emotional availability from parents caught in a trauma bond. This can affect their ability to form healthy relationships later in life.

Role Reversal:
Parentification:
Children often take on roles traditionally associated with adults, such as providing emotional support or mediating conflicts between their trauma bonded parents. This premature role reversal can hinder the child's own emotional development.

Normalization of Dysfunction:
Misinterpretation of Relationships:
Children may perceive the trauma bond between their parents as a normative aspect

of relationships. This normalization can lead them to accept and perpetuate unhealthy dynamics in their own future relationships.

Psychological Distress:
Increased Risk of Mental Health Issues: Exposure to ongoing trauma within the family can contribute to the development of mental health issues in children, including depression, anxiety, and post-traumatic stress disorder (PTSD).

Difficulty Establishing Boundaries:
Lack of Healthy Boundaries: Children growing up in a trauma bond environment may struggle to establish and maintain healthy emotional boundaries. This can result in difficulties asserting themselves and navigating relationships in a balanced way.

Impact on Academic Performance:
Difficulty Concentrating: The emotional turmoil in the household may affect a child's ability to concentrate on academics. Constant exposure to parental conflicts can create a distracting and stressful home environment.

Social Isolation: Reluctance to Form Connections:
Children may be reluctant to form connections with peers or others outside the family due to a fear of judgment or rejection, stemming from the dysfunctional environment at home.

Inability to Express Emotions:
Suppressed Emotional Expression:
Children may learn to suppress their own emotions to avoid adding to the tension at home. This emotional suppression can lead to challenges in understanding and expressing their feelings.

Risk of Replicating Patterns:
Cycle of Dysfunction:
Children raised in a trauma bond environment may be at a higher risk of perpetuating similar patterns in their own relationships, either by seeking out trauma bonded dynamics or by struggling to establish healthy connections.

Intervention and Support:
Therapeutic Assistance: Interventions such as family therapy or individual counseling for the children can help address the impact of living with trauma bonded parents.

Education and Awareness:
Providing education and resources to parents about the effects of trauma bonds and offering support to break free from unhealthy patterns can be crucial.

External Support Networks:
Encouraging children to build relationships with supportive adults or mentors outside the family can offer them alternative perspectives and emotional support. In summary, the impact on children living with parents in a trauma bond relationship is multifaceted, affecting their emotional well-being, social development, and future relationship dynamics. Early intervention, therapeutic support, and a nurturing external environment are essential for breaking the cycle of dysfunction and promoting healthier outcomes for the children involved.

3.3: Parental Relationships:
Trauma bonding in parental relationships refers to the formation of strong emotional connections between a child and a parent, despite the presence of abusive or harmful behavior. This complex and often unconscious bond can develop in situations where a child experiences both moments of affection and care, as well as periods of neglect, emotional abuse, or other forms of mistreatment from a parent. The intermittent reinforcement of positive and negative experiences creates a powerful psychological connection that can be challenging for the child to break, even when the overall relationship is detrimental.

Key aspects of trauma bonding in parental relationships include:

Intermittent Reinforcement:
Trauma bonding involves a cycle of intermittent reinforcement where the parent alternates between periods of affection, love, or care, and episodes of neglect, emotional abuse, or mistreatment. This unpredictability reinforces the child's emotional dependence on the parent.

Dependency and Loyalty:
Despite the harm caused by the parent, the child may develop a strong sense of depen-

dency and loyalty. The child may feel a need to protect the parent or believe that their own well-being is intricately tied to maintaining a connection, even if it is toxic.

Normalization of Abuse:
Over time, the child may internalize the abusive behavior as normal, especially if it has been a consistent part of their upbringing. This normalization can lead to a distorted perception of what constitutes a healthy parent child relationship.

Fear of Abandonment:
The child may fear abandonment or rejection by the parent, even if the parent's actions are harmful. This fear can be a powerful motivator for the child to maintain the connection, despite the associated trauma.

Identity and Self-worth Issues:
Trauma bonding can contribute to the development of identity and self-worth issues in the child. The inconsistent reinforcement of positive and negative experiences may lead to confusion about one's value and place in the world.

Long Term Impact on Relationships:
Children who experience trauma bonding in parental relationships may carry these patterns into their adult relationships. They may struggle with establishing healthy boundaries, recognizing red flags, and may be more susceptible to entering abusive relationships.

Challenges in Breaking the Bond:
Breaking a trauma bond can be extremely challenging for the child, even when they recognize the toxicity of the relationship. Feelings of guilt, shame, and a deep-seated desire for the parent's approval or love can create significant barriers to ending the bond.

Therapeutic Interventions:
Professional therapeutic interventions, such as counseling or psychotherapy, are often necessary to help individuals break free from trauma bonds in parental relationships. Therapists can provide support, validation, and strategies for establishing healthier connections. Addressing trauma bonding in parental relationships requires a multifaceted approach that includes therapeutic support, education, and the development of coping strategies. It is crucial to create an environment where individuals can recognize the impact of the trauma bond, understand its origins, and work towards healing and establishing healthier relationships.

3.4: Cults and Manipulative Groups:

Trauma bonding in cults and manipulative groups involves the formation of strong emotional connections between individuals and the group or its leader, despite the presence of exploitative, coercive, or abusive practices. These bonds are often characterized by a combination of psychological manipulation, control tactics, and the intermittent reinforcement of positive and negative experiences. Understanding trauma bonding in the context of cults and manipulative groups is crucial for comprehending why individuals may stay involved despite the evident harm.

Key aspects of trauma bonding in cults and manipulative groups include:

Love Bombing and Positive Reinforcement:
Cults often employ tactics like love bombing, which involves overwhelming individuals with expressions of love, attention, and validation. This positive reinforcement creates a strong initial bond and sense of belonging.

Isolation and Dependency:
Manipulative groups often isolate individuals from their friends, family, and external support systems. This isolation fosters a sense of dependency on the group for emotional support, identity, and purpose.

Threats and Fear Based Control:
Manipulative leaders may use threats, fear tactics, or punishment to control members. This creates a cycle of fear and relief, with moments of apparent safety and affirmation following periods of coercion.

Cognitive Dissonance:
Members may experience cognitive dissonance, where they hold conflicting beliefs about the group and its practices. To resolve this internal conflict, individuals may downplay or rationalize abusive behaviors, reinforcing their commitment to the group.

Sense of Special Purpose:
Cult leaders often convince followers that they have a unique and special purpose or destiny within the group. This fosters a sense of identity and importance that can be difficult for individuals to relinquish.

Guilt and Shame:
Manipulative groups may use guilt and shame as tools to control members. Individuals may feel responsible for any perceived failures or doubts, reinforcing their commitment to the group to alleviate guilt.

Control of Information:
Cults often control the flow of information, restricting access to external perspectives or critical viewpoints. This control limits members' ability to question the group's teachings or practices.

Groupthink and Conformity:
Cults promote a culture of groupthink and conformity, where dissent or critical thinking is discouraged. Members may fear rejection or ostracization if they express doubts or divergent opinions.

Emotional Manipulation:
Emotional manipulation techniques, such as gaslighting and emotional blackmail, are common in cults. These tactics can lead members to doubt their own perceptions and foster dependence on the group for validation.

Traumatic Rituals:
Some cults use rituals or practices that induce trauma or heightened emotional states. These experiences can create a powerful bond among members who share these intense, often distressing experiences. Breaking free from trauma bonding in cults and manipulative groups is a complex process that often requires external intervention, support from friends and family, and professional counseling. Education about manipulation tactics, understanding the psychology behind these bonds, and providing a safe space for individuals to express their doubts are essential steps in helping individuals disengage from such harmful environments.

3.5: Friendships and Social Circles:
Trauma bonding in friendships and social circles involves the development of strong emotional connections between individuals, often in the presence of shared traumatic experiences or abusive dynamics. These bonds can form in various settings, such as peer groups, social circles, or close friendships, and are characterized by a combination of positive reinforcement, intermittent rewards, and the psychological impact of shared

adversity. Understanding trauma bonding in friendships and social circles is crucial for recognizing the complexity of these relationships and supporting individuals who may be struggling within them.

Key aspects of trauma bonding in friendships and social circles include:

Shared Traumatic Experiences:
Trauma bonding often occurs when individuals in a social circle share traumatic experiences. Whether it's a collective experience of adversity, abuse, or challenging life events, the shared trauma can create a strong emotional connection.

Positive Reinforcement Amidst Adversity:
During times of distress, individuals may provide support, understanding, and comfort to each other. These moments of positive reinforcement within the context of shared adversity contribute to the formation of trauma bonds.Dependency on the Group for Support: Individuals within the social circle may become emotionally dependent on the group for support, validation, and a sense of belonging. This dependency can strengthen the bond and make it challenging for individuals to consider leaving, even if the group dynamics are harmful.

Normalization of Unhealthy Behavior:
Within the social circle, certain behaviors or dynamics that would be considered unhealthy or abusive in other contexts may become normalized. This normalization can make it difficult for individuals to recognize the toxic nature of the relationships.

Fear of Isolation or Rejection:
Individuals in trauma bonded social circles may fear isolation or rejection if they were to distance themselves. This fear can contribute to the maintenance of the bond, as individuals prioritize staying connected over recognizing the negative impact on their well-being.

Power Imbalances and Control:
Power imbalances and control dynamics within the social circle can reinforce the trauma bond. Individuals who hold power or influence may use it to maintain the status quo and discourage dissent or individual autonomy.

Manipulation and Gaslighting:
Manipulative tactics, such as gaslighting, can be present in trauma bonded friendships or social circles. This can lead individuals to doubt their own perceptions, making it challenging for them to recognize and break free from the bond.

Difficulty Setting Boundaries:
Trauma bonded individuals may struggle to set and maintain healthy boundaries within the social circle. The fear of rejection or negative consequences may prevent them from asserting their own needs and well-being.

Impact on Individual Well-being:
Trauma bonding in friendships and social circles can have significant effects on individual mental health, contributing to anxiety, depression, and a sense of entrapment. Recognizing the signs of trauma bonding in friendships and social circles is crucial for offering support and intervention. Encouraging open communication, providing resources for counseling, and fostering a supportive environment can help individuals navigate these complex relationships and work towards healthier social connections.

Chapter Four

Identifying Trauma Bonds

4.1: Recognizing the Signs and Symptoms Emotional Dependence:

Emotional dependence refers to a reliance on others for emotional support, validation, and a sense of self-worth. While interdependence is a natural aspect of healthy relationships, emotional dependence can become problematic when it hinders individual autonomy and well-being. Recognizing signs and symptoms of emotional dependence is important for fostering self-awareness and promoting healthier relationship dynamics.

Here are some common indicators:

Constant Need for Approval:

Individuals who are emotionally dependent often seek constant approval and validation from others. They may base their self-esteem on the opinions and feedback they receive from those around them.

Fear of Abandonment:

A persistent fear of being abandoned or rejected can be a sign of emotional dependence. Individuals may go to great lengths to avoid situations or behaviors that they believe could lead to rejection.

Difficulty Making Decisions Independently:

Emotional dependence may manifest as a reluctance or inability to make decisions without seeking input or approval from others. Individuals may fear making "wrong" choices and look to others to guide their decision making.

Excessive Reliance on a Specific Person:
Emotional dependence often involves an intense reliance on one particular person for emotional support. This person is usually a significant other, friend, or family member, and their approval or presence becomes crucial for the individual's emotional well-being.

Anxiety or Discomfort When Alone:
Individuals who are emotionally dependent may experience heightened anxiety or discomfort when they are alone. The absence of others may lead to feelings of emptiness or insecurity.

Lack of Personal Identity:
Emotional dependence can result in a lack of a distinct personal identity. Individuals may define themselves primarily through their relationships with others, lacking a strong sense of self outside these connections.

Over-reliance on Relationships for Happiness:
Emotional dependence often involves relying solely on relationships for happiness and fulfilment. Individuals may struggle to find satisfaction or contentment independently of their interpersonal connections.

Difficulty Handling Criticism:
Emotional dependence may make it challenging for individuals to handle criticism or disapproval. They may take feedback personally and may go to great lengths to avoid any form of conflict.

Neglect of Personal Goals and Interests:
Individuals who are emotionally dependent may neglect their personal goals, hobbies, and interests in favor of prioritizing the needs and desires of others. Their own aspirations take a backseat to maintaining relationships.

Overwhelming Fear of Rejection:
A pervasive fear of rejection can dominate the thoughts and actions of emotionally dependent individuals. This fear may drive them to compromise their own needs and values to avoid potential rejection.

4.2: Cyclic Patterns of Abuse and Apology:
Cyclic patterns of abuse and apology are characteristic of abusive relationships, where the

abusive partner alternates between harmful behavior and attempts to reconcile through apologies or gestures of remorse. This cyclical pattern, often known as the "cycle of abuse," can create confusion, emotional turmoil, and a sense of dependency in the victim. The cycle typically includes three main phases:

Tension Building Phase:
This phase is marked by increasing tension, stress, and a sense of walking on eggshells. The victim may notice subtle signs of the abuser becoming more agitated or controlling. Communication may become strained, and conflicts may escalate.

Explosion or Acute Abuse Phase:
The tension reaches a breaking point, leading to an explosion of abuse. This can manifest as verbal, emotional, physical, or sexual abuse. The intensity and duration of this phase vary but often involve a loss of control by the abusive partner.

Honeymoon or Reconciliation Phase:
Following the abusive episode, the abuser may express remorse, apologize, and make promises to change. This phase is characterized by efforts to reconcile, with the abuser often displaying kindness, affection, and apologies. The victim may feel relief, hope, and a desire to believe that the abuse will not recur. However, the honeymoon phase is temporary, and the cycle typically repeats, with the tension building phase resuming and leading to another explosion of abuse.

Key features of cyclic patterns of abuse and apology include:

Manipulation and Control:
Abusers use the cycle of abuse to maintain control over their victims. The intermittent reinforcement of abuse and apology can create a sense of unpredictability, making it challenging for the victim to leave the relationship.

Emotional Rollercoaster:
Victims experience a rollercoaster of emotions, ranging from fear and anxiety during the tension building phase, to pain and distress during the acute abuse phase, followed by relief and hope during the reconciliation phase.

Guilt and Shame:
Abusers may exploit the victim's feelings of guilt and shame during the reconciliation

phase, often blaming the victim or external circumstances for the abuse. This manipulation can make it difficult for the victim to hold the abuser accountable.

Cycle Reinforcement:
The cycle of abuse tends to reinforce itself, with each repetition making it more challenging for the victim to break free. Over time, the victim may internalize the cycle and develop a sense of learned helplessness.

Isolation:
Abusers often isolate their victims from friends and family, making it harder for the victim to seek support or perspective outside the abusive relationship. Isolation contributes to the cycle of abuse by limiting external influences.

Escalation Over Time:
The cycle of abuse can escalate over time, with the tension building and acute abuse phases becoming more severe. As the cycle repeats, the likelihood of injury and the emotional toll on the victim may increase. Breaking free from cyclic patterns of abuse and apology often requires external support, such as counseling, advocacy services, and a strong support network. Understanding the dynamics of the cycle is a crucial step for victims in recognizing the need for intervention and seeking help to escape the abusive relationship.

4.3: Isolation from Supportive Networks:
Isolation from supportive networks is a common tactic used by manipulative individuals, abusers, or controlling groups to maintain power and control over their victims. This form of isolation can be emotional, social, or even physical, and it serves to limit the victim's access to external support systems. Here are key aspects of isolation from supportive networks:

Emotional Isolation:
Emotional isolation involves undermining the victim's self-esteem and creating a dependency on the abuser for emotional support. This can be achieved through constant criticism, gaslighting, and diminishing the victim's confidence.

Social Isolation:
Abusers may intentionally isolate their victims from friends, family, or any supportive

social network. This can involve discouraging or preventing contact with loved ones, spreading false information, or creating conflicts to drive a wedge between the victim and their support system.

Control of Communication:
Abusers may control and monitor the victim's communication channels, such as restricting access to phones, monitoring emails or social media, or even preventing the victim from communicating freely. This control limits the victim's ability to reach out for help.

Manipulation of Perceptions:
Abusers often manipulate the victim's perceptions of their friends and family. They may portray loved ones as threats, untrustworthy, or unsupportive, making the victim reluctant to seek help or maintain contact.

Financial Dependence:
Creating financial dependence is another form of isolation. Abusers may control the victim's access to money, employment, or resources, making it difficult for the victim to leave the abusive situation or seek support independently.

Cultural or Religious Isolation:
In some cases, abusers exploit cultural or religious beliefs to isolate victims. They may use cultural norms or religious doctrines to justify the isolation, making it challenging for the victim to challenge or escape the abusive situation.

Physical Confinement:
In extreme cases, physical isolation involves restricting the victim's movement or confining them to a specific space. This can be done through threats, intimidation, or actual physical confinement, making it nearly impossible for the victim to seek help.

Gradual Escalation:
Isolation often occurs gradually, with abusers testing boundaries and gradually cutting off the victim from their support networks over time. This gradual escalation may make it harder for the victim to recognize the extent of the isolation.

Fear and Threats:
Abusers may instill fear in the victim, using threats or intimidation to discourage them

from reaching out for help. The fear of retaliation or harm to themselves or their loved ones may prevent the victim from seeking support.

Undermining Independence:
Abusers may undermine the victim's independence and self-efficacy, making them believe they cannot survive or make decisions without the abuser. This undermines the victim's confidence in their ability to seek help independently. Recognizing signs of isolation is crucial for both victims and those supporting them. Breaking free from isolation often requires external intervention, such as seeking help from friends, family, or support organizations, and developing a safety plan to escape the abusive situation.

4.4: Self-Worth and Identity Issues:
Trauma bonding often manifests in relationships where there is an interplay of intermittent positive experiences and negative, harmful behaviors. This complex dynamic can result in self-worth and identity issues for the individuals involved.

Real-life Examples Illustrating Trauma Bonding:
Case Study: Louisa and Mark – Intimate Relationship:

Background:
Louisa and Mark met in college and fell deeply in love. Their relationship started off strong, but as time went on, Mark's behavior became increasingly controlling and emotionally abusive. Louisa, initially confident and independent, found herself entangled in a web of trauma bonding.

Incidents of Abuse: Isolation Tactics:
Mark gradually isolated Louisa from her friends and family, criticizing them and insisting that he was the only one who truly cared about her.

Emotional Manipulation:
Mark used gaslighting techniques to make Louisa doubt her perceptions and memories. He would deny saying hurtful things or insist that she was overreacting.

Mark's behavior was unpredictable. He would switch between being loving and apologetic to distant and critical. This unpredictability kept Louisa hoping for the return of the person she fell in love with.

Threats and Intimidation:
Mark occasionally used subtle threats, suggesting that Louisa would be alone or worthless without him. This created fear and a sense of dependency.

Trauma Bonding Dynamics:
Cognitive Dissonance:
Louisa experienced conflicting emotions. Despite the abuse, she clung to the positive memories and moments of kindness, creating cognitive dissonance.

Fear of Abandonment:
Louisa feared being alone and believed that she needed Mark for emotional support, even though he was the source of much of her distress.

Hope for Change:
Mark's occasional apologies and moments of kindness fueled Louisa's hope that he would change. She believed that if she loved him enough, he would return to the person he was in the beginning.

Loss of Self Identity:
Louisa's self-esteem eroded over time, and her identity became intertwined with Mark's perception of her. She felt she needed him for validation.

Breaking the Trauma Bond:
Acknowledgment: Louisa began to acknowledge the toxicity of the relationship and the impact on her well-being.

Seeking Support:
Louisa confided in a friend and eventually a therapist, gaining an outside perspective and emotional support.

Setting Boundaries:
With the help of therapy, Louisa started setting boundaries with Mark, insisting on respectful communication, and seeking space when needed.

Developing Independence:
Louisa gradually rebuilt her social connections, pursued her interests, and focused on personal growth.

Conclusion:

Louisa's journey illustrates the complexities of trauma bonding in an intimate relationship. Breaking free required self-awareness, external support, and the courage to redefine her sense of self and reclaim her life. This fictional case study emphasizes the importance of recognizing the signs of trauma bonding and seeking help to break free from a harmful cycle of abuse.

Case Study: Sarah and Lisa – Manipulative Friendship Background:

Sarah and Lisa have been friends since high school. Over the years, their friendship has evolved into a manipulative dynamic, with Lisa exerting subtle control over Sarah's emotions and choices. This case study illustrates the dynamics of trauma bonding within a manipulative friendship.

Incidents of Manipulation:
Subtle Control:
Lisa consistently undermined Sarah's confidence by making dismissive comments about her choices, appearance, and abilities. This behavior was often masked as concern or friendly advice.

Isolation Tactics:
Lisa discouraged Sarah from spending time with other friends, often suggesting that they were not genuine or trustworthy. Over time, Sarah's social circle narrowed, and Lisa became her primary confidante.

Emotional Manipulation:
Lisa frequently played the victim, sharing stories of personal struggles to evoke sympathy from Sarah. This created an emotional dependency, as Sarah felt obligated to support Lisa through her perceived hardships.

Conditional Affection:
Lisa would alternate between being overly supportive and withdrawn based on Sarah's compliance with Lisa's expectations. This created a cycle where Sarah constantly sought Lisa's approval.

Trauma Bonding Dynamics:

Dependency on Approval:
Sarah became overly reliant on Lisa's approval and validation for her self-worth. The conditional nature of Lisa's affection kept Sarah on edge, always striving to meet Lisa's expectations.

Fear of Rejection:
Sarah developed a deep fear of rejection and abandonment. The thought of losing Lisa's friendship created intense anxiety, even when Sarah recognized the toxicity of the relationship.

Sarah often justified Lisa's manipulative actions, attributing them to Lisa's difficult past or stressful circumstances. This allowed the toxic dynamic to persist without questioning.

Cycle of Apologies and Forgiveness:
Lisa would occasionally apologize for her behavior, promising change. Sarah, eager to maintain the friendship, forgave Lisa repeatedly, contributing to the cycle of manipulation.

Breaking the Trauma Bond:
Recognition of Manipulation:
Over time, Sarah started recognizing the manipulative patterns in the friendship, acknowledging the negative impact on her well-being.

Seeking External Perspectives:
Sarah began confiding in other friends and family members, gaining alternative perspectives on healthy relationships, and recognizing the toxic nature of her friendship with Lisa.

Establishing Boundaries:
Sarah started setting boundaries with Lisa, expressing discomfort with certain behaviors, and insisting on maintaining connections with other friends.

Gradual Disengagement:
Sarah slowly distanced herself from Lisa, focusing on rebuilding other friendships and pursuing personal interests outside of the toxic relationship.

Conclusion:

Sarah's experience illustrates how trauma bonding can manifest within a manipulative friendship. Breaking free required self-awareness, seeking external perspectives, and the courage to establish and maintain boundaries. This case study emphasizes the importance of recognizing manipulative dynamics in friendships and taking proactive steps to foster healthy connections.

Case Study: Mia and "The Enlightened Fellowship" – Cult Involvement Background:

Mia, a young professional searching for purpose, joined a spiritual group called "The Enlightened Fellowship." Over time, what initially seemed like a supportive community turned into a cultic environment, and Mia became entangled in a complex web of trauma bonding.

Incidents of Cultic Manipulation:

Love Bombing and Isolation:
Initially, members of the fellowship showered Mia with affection and attention, creating a sense of belonging. However, as the bonding intensified, the group discouraged interactions with non-members, isolating Mia from family and friends.

Guru Worship:
The charismatic leader of the fellowship played a central role in members' lives, portraying themselves as the sole source of spiritual enlightenment. Mia was taught to view the leader as an infallible guide, fostering dependency.

Fear Tactics:
The fellowship used fear inducing messages, predicting dire consequences for those who left the group or questioned the leader's teachings. Mia internalized these fears, leading to a constant state of anxiety.

Conditional Acceptance:
The fellowship provided a sense of acceptance and love, but it was contingent on unquestioning loyalty and adherence to strict rules. Any deviation from the group's norms resulted in emotional manipulation and shaming.

Trauma Bonding Dynamics:

Dependency on the Group:
Mia became emotionally and psychologically dependent on the fellowship for validation, purpose, and a sense of identity. The group's conditional acceptance reinforced the need for conformity.

Fear of Excommunication:
The fear of being cast out from the fellowship and facing the predicted consequences created a strong bond. Mia became deeply fearful of losing the only community they believed truly understood and accepted them.

Cognitive Dissonance:
Despite witnessing questionable practices within the fellowship, Mia suppressed doubts to maintain a sense of security and belonging. The dissonance between critical thoughts and the desire for acceptance contributed to the trauma bond.

Loss of Personal Autonomy:
Over time, Mia relinquished personal autonomy to the group's teachings and the leader's directives. This loss of individuality and critical thinking reinforced the trauma bond.

Breaking the Trauma Bond:

Crisis of Conscience:
A series of incidents within the fellowship raised doubts for Mia, leading to an internal crisis of conscience about the group's true nature.

External Intervention:
Concerned friends, who noticed the changes in Mia's behavior, staged an intervention. They provided information about cult dynamics and encouraged Mia to seek outside perspectives.

Professional Help:
Mia sought the guidance of a cult exit counselor and a mental health professional to navigate the process of disentangling from the trauma bond and recovering from the psychological impact.

Gradual Disengagement:
With support, Mia initiated a gradual disengagement from the fellowship. This included creating physical and emotional distance while building a support network outside the group.

Conclusion:
Mia's experience exemplifies how trauma bonding can occur within the context of cult involvement. Breaking free required a combination of internal questioning, external intervention, and professional support to unravel the complex web of manipulation and rebuild a sense of autonomy and identity. This case study underscores the importance of understanding the dynamics of cultic relationships for both individuals and those aiming to provide support. In each of these examples, the individuals experience trauma bonding as a result of the cyclic patterns of abuse, manipulation, and intermittent positive reinforcement. Over time, their self-worth becomes intertwined with the approval and validation provided by the abusive or controlling figure, leading to a deep sense of dependency and identity issues. Breaking free from trauma bonds often requires external support, self-reflection, and a commitment to rebuilding one's sense of self and worth outside of the toxic relationship or environment.

4.5: Demonstrating Different Contexts of Trauma Bonding:
Here we explain three scenarios to illustrate trauma bonding in different contexts:

Case Study: Maria and her Toxic Workplace Background:
Maria, a dedicated professional, found herself working in a toxic workplace environment that fostered trauma bonding among the employees. The company, driven by a highly demanding and manipulative management style, created a culture where trauma bonding became a prevalent dynamic.

Incidents of Workplace Manipulation: Constant Criticism:
The management routinely criticized employees, focusing on their shortcomings rather than acknowledging their achievements. Maria, despite her competence, felt a constant need to seek validation and approval.

Isolation Tactics:
Employees were discouraged from forming close relationships within the workplace. The management fostered a sense of competition, making it challenging for colleagues to trust

one another. Maria felt isolated and believed that her survival in the workplace depended on staying on the management's good side.

Unrealistic Expectations:
The management set unrealistic expectations and deadlines, creating a perpetual state of stress among employees. They were made to believe that only through unwavering dedication and sacrifices could they prove their loyalty to the company.

Conditional Recognition:
Positive feedback and promotions were granted sparingly and were often tied to employees going above and beyond their regular duties. This created a culture where individuals constantly sought the elusive acknowledgment from the management.

Trauma Bonding Dynamics:
Dependency on Approval:
Maria became dependent on the sporadic approval and positive feedback from the management for her self-worth. The lack of consistent recognition intensified her desire for validation.

Fear of Job Loss:
The constant threat of job insecurity, coupled with the fear of being singled out for criticism, created anxiety and a strong bond among employees. Maria feared losing her job and the financial stability associated with it.

Sense of Collective Suffering:
The shared experience of facing a demanding and manipulative management created a sense of collective suffering among employees. They began to rely on each other for emotional support, reinforcing the bond that developed through shared challenges.

Normalization of Toxicity:
Over time, Maria and her colleagues normalized the toxic behaviors within the workplace. They accepted mistreatment as part of the job, further solidifying the trauma bond by collectively minimizing the severity of the situation.

Breaking the Trauma Bond
Collective Recognition:
A group of employees, including Maria, started recognizing the unhealthy dynamics

within the workplace. They began discussing their experiences openly, realizing that their shared suffering wasn't a normal or acceptable part of professional life.

Whistleblowing and Advocacy:
Some employees decided to blow the whistle on the toxic workplace practices, seeking external intervention. They contacted labor unions, filed complaints with regulatory bodies, and engaged in advocacy efforts to bring attention to the company's unethical practices.

Employee Support Networks:
Maria and her colleagues actively sought support outside the workplace, joining professional networks and seeking guidance from industry mentors. This provided them with alternative perspectives and bolstered their confidence to take action.

Legal Action:
In extreme cases, employees initiated legal action against the company, exposing the toxic workplace culture. This not only brought attention to the company's practices but also facilitated the possibility of compensation for the emotional distress caused.

Conclusion:
Maria's experience demonstrates how trauma bonding can occur in a workplace setting due to manipulative management practices. Breaking free required collective recognition, external intervention, and the courage to challenge the normalization of toxic behaviors. This case study underscores the importance of fostering a healthy work environment and advocating for employee well-being.

Sibling Relationships in a Dysfunctional Family:
Case Study: Jamie and the Dysfunctional Sibling Bond:

Background:
Jamie grew up in a dysfunctional family with parents who struggled with substance abuse and unpredictable behavior. In this challenging environment, a complex trauma bond developed between Jamie and an older sibling, Mia.

Incidents of Family Dysfunction:
Parental Neglect:
Both Jamie and Mia experienced emotional and physical neglect from their parents, who

were often consumed by their own issues. This lack of consistent care created a deep emotional void for both siblings.

Siblings as Allies:
In the absence of parental support, Jamie and Mia became allies in navigating the chaos at home. They formed a close bond as they leaned on each other for emotional support and protection from the unpredictable behavior of their parents.

Enabling Behavior:
Mia, being the older sibling, took on a protective role for Jamie. However, this protective stance often involved enabling unhealthy coping mechanisms, such as substance use, to cope with the family's dysfunction.

Cycle of Dysfunction:
The dysfunctional family dynamics created a cycle of chaos, where both siblings found themselves repeating patterns of neglect, emotional instability, and unhealthy coping mechanisms learned from their parents.

Trauma Bonding Dynamics:
Mutual Dependency:
Jamie and Mia developed a mutual dependency, relying on each other for emotional comfort and stability in the absence of reliable parental support.

Shared Secrets:
The siblings harbored shared secrets about the dysfunction within their family. This created a bond founded on a shared understanding of the challenges they faced, fostering a sense of loyalty.

Protective Instincts:
Mia's protective instincts, while well intentioned, contributed to a sense of indebtedness in Jamie. Jamie felt obligated to reciprocate this protection by maintaining loyalty to Mia, even when it involved engaging in destructive behaviors.

Normalization of Dysfunction:
Over time, Jamie and Mia normalized the dysfunctional family dynamics. They found comfort in their shared experiences, despite the inherent toxicity, creating a reluctance to challenge or break free from the trauma bond.

Breaking the Trauma Bond:
Therapeutic Intervention:
Both Jamie and Mia sought individual therapy to address the impact of their dysfunctional upbringing. Through therapy, they gained insights into how their trauma bond was affecting their personal growth and relationships.

Establishing Healthy Boundaries:
With the guidance of therapists, Jamie and Mia worked on establishing healthy boundaries in their relationship. This involved recognizing and challenging enabling behaviors and fostering independence.

Individual Growth:
Jamie and Mia embarked on individual journeys of self-discovery and personal growth. They pursued interests and formed relationships outside their sibling bond, reducing the exclusive dependency on each other.

Family Interventions:
Recognizing the need for a healthier family environment, Jamie and Mia advocated for family interventions, including seeking support for their parents' substance abuse issues. This collective effort aimed to break the cycle of dysfunction for the entire family.

Conclusion:
Jamie's experience highlights how trauma bonding can manifest in a sibling relationship within a dysfunctional family. Breaking free required therapeutic intervention, the establishment of healthy boundaries, individual growth, and collective efforts to address the root causes of the family dysfunction. This case study emphasizes the importance of seeking external support to disrupt harmful patterns and foster a healthier family dynamic. These scenarios demonstrate the versatility of trauma bonding across different contexts, highlighting that it can occur in various relationships and environments. The underlying theme is the cyclic pattern of abusive behavior followed by intermittent positive reinforcement, leading individuals to form deep emotional connections that are difficult to break.

Chapter Five

Breaking the Chains

Self-awareness and Acknowledgment:
Self-awareness and acknowledgment are crucial steps in recognizing the existence of a trauma bond. Acknowledging and understanding the dynamics of a trauma bond can be challenging, but it is a necessary and empowering process for breaking free from unhealthy relationships. Here are steps to increase self-awareness and acknowledge a trauma bond:

Recognizing the Existence of a Trauma Bond:
Educate Yourself:
Learn about trauma bonding and its characteristics. Understand the patterns of abuse, intermittent reinforcement, and the psychological impact on individuals. Education can empower you to recognize these patterns in your own relationships.

Reflect on Relationship Patterns:
Take time to reflect on your relationship dynamics. Consider the cycles of tension, acute abuse, and reconciliation. Identify instances of positive reinforcement that follow periods of mistreatment. Reflecting on your experiences can provide valuable insights into the nature of the relationship.

Journaling:
Keep a journal to document your feelings, experiences, and observations within the relationship. Writing down your thoughts can help clarify your emotions and provide a record of the cyclic patterns that may be indicative of a trauma bond.

Seek External Perspectives:
Share your experiences with trusted friends, family members, or a therapist. Seeking external perspectives can provide valuable insights and help you gain a clearer understanding of the dynamics in your relationship. Others may offer observations that you might not have considered.

Trust Your Instincts:
Pay attention to your gut feelings and instincts. If you consistently feel uneasy, anxious, or trapped in the relationship, it may be an indication of a trauma bond. Trusting your instincts is an important aspect of self-awareness.

Recognize the Impact on Well-being:
Acknowledge the impact of the relationship on your mental, emotional, and physical well-being. Assess whether the relationship is contributing positively to your life or if it is causing distress, anxiety, or harm.

Evaluate Dependency and Fear:
Assess your dependency on the relationship and whether fear plays a significant role in your decision making. If the fear of abandonment, rejection, or retaliation is a driving force in maintaining the connection, it may be indicative of a trauma bond.

Explore Past Patterns:
Reflect on past relationships and patterns. If you notice a recurring theme of trauma bonds or unhealthy dynamics, it may be helpful to explore the root causes and commonalities in these relationships.

Consider Professional Support:
Engage the support of a mental health professional, such as a therapist or counselor. They can provide guidance, support, and tools to help you navigate the complexities of trauma bonding and work towards breaking free from unhealthy relationships.

Commit to Self-care:
Prioritize self-care and self-compassion. Recognize that breaking free from a trauma bond is a process that requires time and effort. Focus on activities that promote your well-being and build a positive self-image. Acknowledging a trauma bond is a significant step towards breaking free from its grip. By increasing self-awareness, seeking support, and taking

intentional steps towards healing, individuals can empower themselves to create healthier, more fulfilling relationships.

5.1: Understanding Personal Triggers:
Understanding personal triggers is a crucial aspect of self-awareness and emotional intelligence. Recognizing what triggers certain emotional responses allows you to navigate your reactions more effectively and implement coping strategies. Here are steps to enhance your self-awareness in understanding personal triggers:

Reflect on Emotional Responses:
Take time to reflect on your emotional responses in various situations. Identify moments when you felt particularly strong emotions such as anger, sadness, anxiety, or frustration. Consider the circumstances, people involved, and your reactions.

Keep a Trigger Journal:
Maintain a trigger journal where you document situations that evoke strong emotional responses. Note the details surrounding each trigger, including the environment, people, and specific events. This journal can serve as a tool for pattern recognition.

Identify Patterns and Themes:
Review your trigger journal periodically to identify patterns or common themes. Are there recurring situations or specific types of interactions that consistently trigger emotional responses? Recognizing patterns can provide insights into underlying triggers.

Explore Childhood and Past Experiences:
Consider your childhood and past experiences that may have contributed to the development of certain triggers. Traumatic events, unresolved issues, or early conditioning can shape emotional responses in adulthood. Understanding the roots of triggers is essential for healing.

Connect Triggers to Core Beliefs:
Examine the core beliefs or narratives you hold about yourself, others, and the world. Triggers often stem from these deep-seated beliefs. For example, if you have a belief of not being worthy of love, situations that challenge your perceived worthiness may trigger strong emotional reactions.

Observe Physical Sensations:
Pay attention to physical sensations accompanying emotional triggers. Notice changes in your body, such as tension, rapid heartbeat, or shallow breathing. Understanding the physiological aspects of triggers can enhance self-awareness.

Ask for Feedback:
Seek feedback from trusted friends, family members, or colleagues. Others may observe patterns or triggers that you might not be fully aware of. A different perspective can provide valuable insights into your behavior.

Mindfulness and Meditation:
Practice mindfulness and meditation to increase awareness of the present moment. Mindfulness techniques can help you observe your thoughts and emotions without judgment, allowing you to identify triggers and choose more intentional responses.

Therapeutic Support:
Consider seeking the support of a therapist or counselor. Professional guidance can help you explore deep seated triggers, understand their origins, and develop coping strategies to manage emotional responses more effectively.

Develop Coping Strategies:
Once you've identified triggers, work on developing coping strategies. This might include deep breathing exercises, positive affirmations, cognitive restructuring, or engaging in activities that bring comfort and relaxation.

Create a Wellness Plan:
Develop a comprehensive wellness plan that incorporates strategies for self-care, stress reduction, and emotional regulation. A well-rounded plan can support your efforts in managing triggers and maintaining emotional balance. Understanding personal triggers is an ongoing process that requires self-reflection, openness, and a commitment to personal growth. By increasing awareness and implementing effective coping strategies, you empower yourself to navigate challenging emotions and foster overall well-being.

5.2 Seeking Professional Help Therapeutic Approaches:
Cognitive Behavioral Therapy (CBT)
Cognitive Behavioral Therapy (CBT) is a widely used therapeutic approach that focuses on the connection between thoughts, feelings, and behaviors. It is a goal oriented and time

limited form of psychotherapy that aims to help individuals identify and change negative thought patterns and behaviors.

Here are key components and principles of Cognitive Behavioral Therapy:

Cognitive Restructuring:
CBT involves identifying and challenging negative or irrational thought patterns. Therapists work with individuals to reframe distorted thinking and replace negative thoughts with more balanced and realistic ones.

Behavioral Activation:
This component emphasizes the connection between thoughts and behaviors. Individuals learn to identify and modify behaviors that contribute to negative emotions. Behavioral activation involves setting specific, achievable goals to increase positive activities and reduce avoidance behaviors.

Mindfulness and Relaxation Techniques:
CBT often incorporates mindfulness and relaxation strategies to help individuals stay present in the moment, manage stress, and reduce anxiety. Mindfulness techniques involve paying attention to thoughts and feelings without judgment.

Homework Assignments:
CBT typically includes homework assignments between sessions. These assignments may involve practicing new skills, keeping thought records, or engaging in specific behaviors to reinforce therapeutic goals.

Goal Setting:
CBT is goal oriented, and individuals work with therapists to set specific, measurable, achievable, relevant, and time bound (SMART) goals. This collaborative approach encourages active participation in the therapeutic process.

Identifying Cognitive Distortions:
Therapists help individuals recognize common cognitive distortions, such as black and white thinking, catastrophizing, or personalization. By identifying and challenging these distortions, individuals gain a more balanced perspective on situations.

Graded Exposure:
For individuals facing anxiety or phobias, CBT may involve graded exposure. This technique gradually exposes individuals to feared situations or stimuli, allowing them to confront and overcome their fears in a controlled and systematic manner.

Problem Solving Skills:
CBT equips individuals with problem solving skills to cope with life stressors. This involves breaking down problems into manageable parts, generating potential solutions, and evaluating their effectiveness.

Collaborative and Empathetic Therapeutic Relationship:
The therapeutic relationship in CBT is collaborative, with therapists working together with individuals to set goals and develop strategies for change. Therapists provide support, encouragement, and empathy while challenging unhelpful thought patterns.

Relapse Prevention:
CBT often includes relapse prevention strategies. Individuals learn to recognize early signs of relapse, develop coping mechanisms, and create plans to maintain progress beyond the conclusion of therapy.

Group and Individual Formats:
CBT can be delivered in individual or group formats, depending on the needs and preferences of the individual. Group CBT can provide additional benefits such as social support and shared experiences. Cognitive Behavioral Therapy has been extensively researched and is effective in treating a range of mental health conditions, including anxiety disorders, depression, post-traumatic stress disorder (PTSD), and various behavioral issues. It is a structured and practical approach that empowers individuals to develop coping skills and make lasting changes in their lives.

Dialectical Behavior Therapy (DBT):
Dialectical Behavior Therapy (DBT) is a therapeutic approach developed by Dr. Marsha M. Linehan. Initially designed to treat individuals with borderline personality disorder (BPD), DBT has proven effective for various mental health conditions characterized by emotional dysregulation and difficulties in interpersonal relationships. DBT incorporates cognitive behavioral techniques and Eastern mindfulness practices.

Here are key components and principles of Dialectical Behavior Therapy:

Dialectics:

DBT is based on dialectical philosophy, which emphasizes the integration of opposing concepts. In therapy, dialectics involve finding a balance between acceptance and change, validation and change, and the dialectic between the therapist's and client's perspectives.

Mindfulness Skills:

Mindfulness is a central component of DBT. It involves paying attention to the present moment without judgment. Individuals learn mindfulness skills to increase awareness, regulate emotions, and cultivate a non-judgmental stance toward themselves and their experiences.

Distress Tolerance:

Distress tolerance skills help individuals cope with crises and intense emotions without resorting to destructive behaviors. Techniques include distraction, self-soothing activities, and acceptance of the current situation.

Emotion Regulation:

DBT focuses on enhancing emotional regulation skills. Individuals learn to identify and label their emotions, understand the functions of emotions, and develop strategies to modulate intense emotional responses.

Interpersonal Effectiveness:

Interpersonal effectiveness skills in DBT involve learning assertiveness, setting boundaries, and effectively expressing needs in relationships. The goal is to improve communication and build healthier interpersonal connections.

Middle Path Skills:

DBT emphasizes finding a middle path between extreme positions. This involves balancing acceptance and change, validation, and encouragement, and maintaining an effective, non-extreme stance in challenging situations.

Validation:

Therapists using DBT actively validate clients' thoughts, feelings, and experiences. Validation helps individuals feel understood and accepted, fostering a collaborative and supportive therapeutic relationship.

Chain Analysis:

Chain analysis is a tool used in DBT to examine the sequence of events leading up to a problematic behavior. It helps individuals understand the chain of events, thoughts, and emotions that contribute to maladaptive behaviors, facilitating more effective problem solving.

Diary Cards:

Clients often keep diary cards to track emotions, behaviors, and skills practice between therapy sessions. Diary cards provide a visual record of progress, patterns, and areas for further skill development.

Commitment to Therapy:

In DBT, individuals commit to therapy and work collaboratively with the therapist to achieve treatment goals. Commitment involves actively participating in sessions, completing homework assignments, and practicing new skills in daily life.

Phone Coaching:

DBT may include phone coaching, allowing clients to reach out to therapists between sessions for support and guidance during crises or challenging situations. Phone coaching reinforces skill utilization in real life scenarios. Dialectical Behavior Therapy has been adapted for various mental health issues beyond BPD, including mood disorders, eating disorders, and substance use disorders. Its comprehensive approach addresses a range of skills needed for emotional regulation, interpersonal effectiveness, and overall well-being. DBT is typically delivered in individual therapy, skills training groups, and phone coaching sessions.

Eye Movement Desensitization and Reprocessing (EMDR):

Eye Movement Desensitization and Reprocessing (EMDR) is a therapeutic approach developed by Dr. Francine Shapiro in the late 1980s. Initially designed to treat post-traumatic stress disorder (PTSD), EMDR has since been used to address a range of psychological issues. The method involves a structured eight phase approach, incorporating bilateral stimulation, such as side to side eye movements, auditory tones, or tactile stimulation.

Here are key components and principles of Eye Movement:

Desensitization and Reprocessing: Assessment and Treatment Planning:

The therapist and client collaboratively assess the client's history, current symptoms, and treatment goals. Treatment planning involves identifying specific target memories or experiences to process during EMDR.

Desensitization:
Desensitization is a core component of EMDR. It involves reprocessing distressing memories, reducing the emotional charge associated with them, and facilitating adaptive resolution. Bilateral stimulation, often in the form of side-to-side eye movements, is used during this phase.

Installation:
Installation focuses on enhancing positive beliefs and self-esteem. Adaptive cognitions are identified, and the therapist guides the client in reinforcing these positive beliefs while continuing bilateral stimulation.

Body Scan:
The body scan phase involves identifying and processing any residual physical tension or discomfort associated with the targeted memory. The goal is to ensure that the entire memory network is addressed, including any somatic sensations.

Closure:
Closure occurs at the end of each EMDR session. The therapist guides the client in stabilizing and grounding themselves. The client is encouraged to use self-soothing techniques between sessions to manage any residual emotions.

Re-evaluation:
Re-evaluation takes place at the beginning of each subsequent session. The therapist and client reassess the client's progress and identify any new targets for processing. This ongoing assessment ensures that all relevant memories are addressed.

Bilateral Stimulation:
Bilateral stimulation is a key element of EMDR. While the client focuses on a target memory or thought, the therapist introduces bilateral stimuli, such as the movement of the therapist's fingers, tapping, or auditory tones. This bilateral stimulation is thought to facilitate the processing of distressing memories.

Adaptive Information Processing (AIP) Model:
The AIP model is the theoretical foundation of EMDR. It posits that distressing mem-

ories are inadequately processed and stored, leading to emotional dysregulation. EMDR aims to facilitate the adaptive processing of these memories, allowing the individual to integrate them more healthily.

Resource Development and Installation (RDI):
RDI involves enhancing clients' internal resources to cope with distress. Positive memories or strengths are identified, and the therapist guides the client in processing these resources using bilateral stimulation.

Targeting Past, Present, and Future:
EMDR can be applied to distressing memories from the past, current stressors, and anticipated future challenges. The flexibility of the approach allows it to address a range of psychological issues beyond trauma.

Adherence to Standardized Protocols:
EMDR therapists follow standardized protocols to ensure consistency and effectiveness. These protocols guide the therapist through the eight phases of treatment, emphasizing the importance of maintaining a structured and systematic approach. EMDR has demonstrated efficacy in treating trauma related disorders, anxiety, depression, and various other psychological conditions. While the mechanism of action is not fully understood, research suggests that EMDR helps individuals reprocess traumatic memories, reducing their emotional impact and facilitating adaptive resolution.

5.3: Support Groups and Communities:
The Importance of Peer Support:
Peer support plays a crucial role in fostering the well-being and recovery of individuals facing various challenges, including mental health issues, chronic illnesses, addiction, trauma, and more. The importance of peer support is multi-faceted and extends across different aspects of an individual's life.

Here are key reasons why peer support is invaluable:

Shared Understanding and Empathy:
Peers who have experienced similar challenges can provide a unique level of understanding and empathy. They share common experiences, allowing for a deeper connection and a sense that one is not alone in their struggles.

Validation and Affirmation:
Peer support offers validation and affirmation of individuals' experiences, feelings, and concerns. Feeling understood and acknowledged by peers can counteract feelings of isolation and contribute to improved self-esteem.

Reducing Stigma and Isolation:
Peer support helps break down stigma by fostering open conversations about mental health, addiction, and other challenges. By creating a supportive community, individuals feel less isolated and are more likely to seek help without fear of judgment.

Role Modeling and Hope:
Peers who have overcome similar challenges serve as role models, offering hope and inspiration to those currently facing difficulties. Seeing others successfully navigate their journeys provides encouragement and a belief that recovery is possible.

Practical Advice and Coping Strategies:
Peer support groups provide a platform for sharing practical advice, coping strategies, and effective solutions. Individuals can learn from the experiences of others and gain valuable insights into managing their challenges.

Shared Resources and Information:
Peers often share resources, information, and recommendations related to treatment options, therapy approaches, self-help tools, and community services. This collective knowledge can empower individuals to make informed decisions about their well-being.

Emotional Support During Crises:
Peer support is particularly valuable during crises or challenging moments. Knowing that others have faced similar difficulties and come through them can provide a sense of comfort, reassurance, and emotional stability.

Building a Sense of Community:
Peer support groups create a sense of community and belonging. This communal aspect fosters social connections and helps individuals build a network of supportive relationships outside their immediate family or friend circles.

Enhanced Motivation and Accountability:
The encouragement and accountability provided by peers can enhance motivation for

personal growth and recovery. Knowing that others are cheering for one's progress can be a powerful motivator.

Promoting Active Participation:
Peer support encourages active participation in one's recovery or personal development. It empowers individuals to take charge of their well-being and engage in strategies that contribute to positive outcomes.

Long Term Recovery and Wellness:
Peer support is not only beneficial during acute phases but also contributes to long term recovery and wellness. The ongoing support from a peer community helps individuals sustain positive changes and navigate the challenges that may arise over time. Peer support can take various forms, including support groups, online communities, mentoring programs, and one on one connections. It offers a holistic approach to well-being, addressing not only the symptoms of a specific challenge but also the emotional, social, and practical aspects of an individual's life.

Chapter Six

Rebuilding and Healing

6.1: Establishing Healthy Boundaries Recognizing and Communicating Boundaries:

Rebuilding and healing often involve the establishment of healthy boundaries in various aspects of life. Healthy boundaries are essential for maintaining emotional well-being, fostering positive relationships, and ensuring personal growth.

Here are key steps in recognizing, communicating, and establishing healthy boundaries:

Self-Reflection:

Take time for self-reflection to identify your needs, values, and limits. Understand what makes you feel comfortable or uncomfortable in different situations. This self-awareness is the foundation for establishing healthy boundaries.

Identify Personal Boundaries:

Clearly define your personal boundaries in different areas of life, including relationships, work, and self-care. Consider your emotional, physical, and time related boundaries. This clarity helps you communicate your expectations to others.

Understand Limits and Tolerance:

Recognize your limits and tolerance levels for various behaviors or situations. Understanding what you can and cannot tolerate allows you to set realistic and effective boundaries that prioritize your well-being.

Acknowledge Past Violations:
Reflect on past experiences where your boundaries were violated. Understand how these experiences have impacted you and use them as lessons for setting clearer boundaries in the future.

Learn to Say No:
Practice saying no assertively when needed. Saying no is a fundamental aspect of establishing boundaries. It's important to express your limits without guilt and to prioritize your own needs.

Communicate Clearly and Directly:
Clearly communicate your boundaries to others. Be direct and assertive in expressing your needs and expectations. Avoid vague or ambiguous language to ensure understanding.

Use "I" Statements:
Frame your boundary setting using "I" statements to convey your feelings and needs without blaming others. For example, say "I feel overwhelmed when..." instead of "You always make me feel overwhelmed."

Be Consistent:
Consistency is key in maintaining healthy boundaries. Be consistent in both setting and enforcing your boundaries. This helps establish a clear understanding of your expectations.

Monitor Your Comfort Level:
Pay attention to your emotions and comfort level in different situations. If you start feeling uncomfortable or overwhelmed, it may be a sign that your boundaries are being tested or violated.

Reinforce Boundaries as Needed:
Periodically reassess and reinforce your boundaries based on changes in your life or relationships. As circumstances evolve, it's important to adjust your boundaries accordingly.

Seek Support:
Share your boundary setting goals with supportive friends, family, or a therapist. Having a support system can provide encouragement and guidance as you work to establish and maintain healthy boundaries.

Practice Self-care:
Prioritize self-care to nurture your overall well-being. Setting boundaries around personal time, self-care practices, and rest is crucial for maintaining physical and emotional health.

Be Mindful of Others' Boundaries:
Respect the boundaries of others as you establish your own. Recognizing and respecting mutual boundaries is key to fostering healthy and reciprocal relationships.

Seek Professional Guidance:
If setting boundaries proves challenging or if past experiences have left deep emotional scars, consider seeking the support of a therapist or counselor. Professional guidance can provide insights and tools for establishing healthier boundaries.

Celebrate Progress:
Acknowledge and celebrate your progress in establishing and maintaining healthy boundaries. Recognize the positive impact it has on your well-being and relationships. Establishing and communicating healthy boundaries is an ongoing process that contributes significantly to personal growth and healing. It empowers individuals to create environments that support their emotional, physical, and relational needs while fostering a sense of self respect and dignity.

Importance of Consistency:
Consistency in self-care practices is crucial for maintaining physical well-being and overall health. Establishing and adhering to a routine of self-care activities contributes to a balanced and sustainable lifestyle. Here's why consistency in self-care practices is important, particularly for physical well-being:

6.2: Self-Care Practices:
Physical Well-being:

Prevention of Burnout:
Consistent self-care practices help prevent burnout by allowing individuals to recharge

and rejuvenate regularly. Taking breaks, getting adequate sleep, and engaging in leisure activities are essential components of preventing physical and emotional exhaustion.

Stress Reduction:
Regular self-care activities, such as mindfulness exercises, deep breathing, or hobbies, contribute to stress reduction. Consistency in practicing stress management techniques helps maintain lower stress levels, which, in turn, positively impacts physical health.

Improved Sleep Quality:
Consistent bedtime routines and sleep hygiene practices contribute to improved sleep quality. Quality sleep is crucial for physical recovery, immune function, and overall well-being.

Enhanced Physical Health:
Regular physical activity and exercise are key components of self-care. Consistency in incorporating exercise into your routine promotes cardiovascular health, strength, flexibility, and helps manage weight.

Optimal Nutrition:
Consistent and balanced eating habits contribute to optimal nutrition. Eating a well-rounded diet with a variety of nutrients supports overall physical health, energy levels, and immune function.

Mental and Emotional Resilience:
Regular self-care practices, including activities that promote mental and emotional well-being, build resilience. Consistency in activities like meditation, journaling, or therapy helps individuals cope with challenges and maintain a positive mindset.

Establishment of Healthy Habits:
Consistency is key to forming and maintaining healthy habits. Whether it's regular exercise, nutritious eating, or getting enough sleep, repeated actions contribute to the establishment of habits that support physical well-being.

Balanced Energy Levels:
Consistent self-care practices help maintain balanced energy levels throughout the day. Adequate rest, hydration, and breaks contribute to sustained energy and prevent energy crashes.

Prevention of Health Issues:
By consistently engaging in preventive health measures, such as regular checkups, screenings, and vaccinations, individuals can proactively address potential health issues before they become serious.

Enhanced Immune Function:
Adequate sleep, proper nutrition, and stress management contribute to a robust immune system. Consistency in these self-care practices helps the body defend against illnesses and infections.

Improved Focus and Productivity:
Taking breaks and engaging in self-care activities improves focus and productivity. Consistently incorporating short breaks throughout the day contributes to better concentration and cognitive function.

Positive Impact on Long Term Health:
The cumulative effect of consistent self-care practices over time has a positive impact on long term health. It helps prevent chronic health conditions and supports overall longevity.

Fostering a Positive Relationship with the Body:
Consistent self-care practices promote a positive relationship with the body. Regular exercise, proper nutrition, and adequate rest contribute to a sense of body positivity and overall well-being.

Increased Quality of Life:
Consistency in self-care practices leads to an increased quality of life. Physical well-being is interconnected with emotional, mental, and social well-being, contributing to a more fulfilling and balanced life.

Setting a Foundation for Holistic Wellness:
Consistent self-care practices contribute to holistic wellness by addressing physical, emotional, mental, and social aspects of health. This comprehensive approach sets a foundation for overall well-being.

In summary, consistency in self-care practices is a foundational aspect of maintaining physical well-being. By incorporating regular routines and activities that support health, individuals can enhance their resilience, prevent burnout, and foster a positive and sustainable approach to life.

6.3: Emotional and Psychological Well-being:

Emotional and psychological well-being are integral aspects of overall health, encompassing a person's mental, emotional, and social states. Achieving and maintaining well-being in these areas contributes to a fulfilling and balanced life.

Here are key components and practices that promote emotional and psychological well-being:

Self-awareness:

Develop self-awareness to understand your thoughts, feelings, and behaviors. Reflect on your values, strengths, and areas for growth. Increased self-awareness lays the foundation for effective emotional regulation.

Emotional Regulation:

Learn and practice healthy ways to regulate your emotions. This includes identifying and expressing emotions, coping with stress, and developing resilience in the face of challenges.

Positive Relationships:

Cultivate positive relationships with family, friends, and a supportive social network. Healthy connections provide emotional support, companionship, and a sense of belonging.

Effective Communication:

Develop effective communication skills to express your thoughts and feelings assertively. Clear communication fosters understanding and helps build positive relationships.

Mindfulness and Present Moment Awareness:

Practice mindfulness to stay present in the moment and cultivate awareness. Mindfulness techniques, such as meditation and deep breathing, can reduce stress and promote emotional well-being.

Work Life Balance:
Strive for a healthy balance between work, personal life, and leisure activities. Maintaining balance contributes to reduced stress and increased overall life satisfaction.

Resilience:
Cultivate resilience to bounce back from setbacks and challenges. Embrace a growth mindset that views difficulties as opportunities for learning and personal development.

Purpose and Meaning:
Identify and pursue activities that provide a sense of purpose and meaning. Engaging in activities aligned with your values contributes to a sense of fulfillment and psychological well-being.

Gratitude Practices:
Foster gratitude by regularly acknowledging and appreciating positive aspects of your life. Gratitude practices have been linked to improved mental health and overall well-being.

Self-Compassion:
Be kind and compassionate toward yourself. Practice self-compassion by acknowledging your imperfections without harsh self-judgment. Treat yourself with the same kindness you would offer a friend.

Healthy Lifestyle Choices:
Adopt a healthy lifestyle, including regular exercise, balanced nutrition, and sufficient sleep. Physical well-being is closely connected to emotional and psychological health.

Seeking Support:
Don't hesitate to seek support when needed. Reach out to friends, family, or mental health professionals. Seeking support is a sign of strength and a proactive step toward well-being.

Positive Distractions and Hobbies:
Engage in positive distractions and hobbies that bring joy and fulfillment. Creative activities, hobbies, and leisure pursuits contribute to a sense of well-being.

Setting Boundaries:
Establish and maintain healthy boundaries in relationships and work. Setting boundaries protects your well-being and helps maintain a balance between giving and receiving.

Continuous Learning and Growth:
Embrace a mindset of continuous learning and personal growth. Challenge yourself, pursue new interests, and explore opportunities for development.

Therapeutic Support:
If needed, consider seeking therapeutic support from a counselor or psychologist. Professional guidance can provide valuable tools and insights for navigating emotional and psychological challenges.

Mind Body Connection:
Recognize the connection between the mind and body. Practices such as yoga, tai chi, or progressive muscle relaxation can promote relaxation and overall well-being.

Cognitive Behavioral Strategies:
Learn and apply cognitive behavioral strategies to address negative thought patterns and behaviors. Cognitive behavioral therapy (CBT) techniques can be effective in promoting positive mental health.

Social Connection:
Nurture social connections by spending quality time with loved ones, participating in group activities, or joining communities with shared interests. Social connections are essential for emotional well-being.

Celebrating Achievements:
Acknowledge and celebrate your achievements, no matter how small. Recognizing your accomplishments boosts self-esteem and contributes to a positive mindset. Promoting emotional and psychological well-being is an ongoing process that involves intentional practices, self-reflection, and a commitment to personal growth. Integrating these elements into your daily life contributes to a more resilient, balanced, and fulfilling emotional and psychological state.

6.4: Building a Supportive Network:
Building a supportive network, fostering empowerment, and setting goals for the future

are interconnected aspects of personal development that contribute to a fulfilling and resilient life. Here's a guide on how to approach each of these elements:

Identify Positive Influences:
Identify individuals who inspire, motivate, and support you. These can be friends, family members, mentors, or colleagues who contribute positively to your life.

Cultivate Healthy Relationships:
Nurture healthy relationships by fostering open communication, mutual respect, and trust. Surround yourself with people who uplift and encourage you.

Join Communities:
Engage in communities or groups with shared interests. Whether online or in person, being part of a community provides a sense of belonging and a platform for shared experiences.

Seek Diversity in Relationships:
Build a diverse network with individuals from different backgrounds, perspectives, and experiences. Diversity enriches your support system and exposes you to varied insights.
Reciprocal Support: Foster reciprocal support within your network. Be willing to offer support to others as well. A supportive network is built on mutual care and encouragement.

Establish Boundaries:
Set and communicate boundaries within your relationships. Healthy boundaries ensure that your interactions are respectful and supportive, preventing potential stressors.

Quality over Quantity:
Focus on the quality of relationships rather than quantity. A few genuine, supportive connections can have a more significant impact on your well-being than a large but superficial network.

Regular Check Ins:
Stay connected with your support network through regular check ins. These can be casual conversations, scheduled catch ups, or virtual meetings. Consistent communication strengthens relationships.

Empowerment and Personal Growth:

Self-Reflection:

Engage in self-reflection to identify your strengths, values, and areas for growth. Understanding yourself is the first step toward empowerment.

Set Personal Goals:

Define personal goals that align with your values and aspirations. Break them down into smaller, achievable steps. Goal setting provides direction and purpose.

Embrace Challenges:

View challenges as opportunities for learning and growth. Embracing challenges with a positive mindset fosters resilience and empowerment.

Continuous Learning:

Commit to continuous learning. Whether through formal education, workshops, or self-directed learning, acquiring new skills and knowledge enhances your sense of empowerment.

Practice Self Compassion:

Be kind to yourself and practice self-compassion. Acknowledge your achievements, learn from setbacks, and treat yourself with the same kindness you would offer a friend.

Assertiveness:

Develop assertiveness in communication. Clearly express your thoughts, needs, and boundaries. Assertiveness fosters self-empowerment and enhances interpersonal relationships.

Expand Comfort Zones:

Challenge yourself to step outside your comfort zones. Growth often occurs when you embrace new experiences, even if they initially seem intimidating.

Celebrate Achievements:

Celebrate both small and significant achievements. Recognizing your accomplishments boosts self-confidence and reinforces a positive sense of self.

Setting Goals for the Future:

Define Short Term and Long-Term Goals:
Clearly define both short term and long-term goals. Short term goals provide immediate direction, while long term goals contribute to a vision for the future.

Align with Values:
Ensure that your goals align with your values and aspirations. Authentic goals are more motivating and contribute to a sense of fulfilment.

Create Action Plans:
Break down each goal into actionable steps. Create a detailed action plan that outlines the specific tasks required to achieve your objectives.

Stay Flexible:
While planning is crucial, remain flexible in your approach. Life is dynamic, and being adaptable allows you to navigate unexpected challenges.

Seek Feedback:
Share your goals with trusted individuals in your support network. Seek feedback and guidance to refine your goals and ensure they are realistic and achievable.

Measure Progress:
Regularly assess your progress toward your goals. Celebrate milestones and adjust your approach if needed. Monitoring progress provides motivation and direction.

Reassess and Update:
Periodically reassess your goals and update them based on changes in your priorities, values, or circumstances. Your goals should evolve as you grow.

Visualize Success:
Use visualization techniques to imagine yourself achieving your goals. Visualization can enhance motivation and help overcome obstacles along the way.

Celebrate Endings and Beginnings:
Celebrate the accomplishment of goals and acknowledge the end of one chapter before embracing new beginnings. Reflect on what you've learned and carry those lessons forward. Building a supportive network, fostering empowerment, and setting goals are

ongoing processes that contribute to a sense of purpose, resilience, and well-being. By intentionally investing in these areas, you create a foundation for personal growth and a more fulfilling future.

Chapter Seven

Preventing Future Bonds

7.1: Education and Awareness: - Recognizing Potential Red Flags:
Recognizing Potential Red Flags in Relationships Recognizing red flags is crucial for maintaining healthy and positive relationships. Identifying warning signs early on allows individuals to make informed decisions and take steps to address potential issues. Here are common red flags that may indicate unhealthy dynamics in relationships:

Lack of Communication:
Consistent communication breakdown, avoidance of important topics, or refusal to engage in open and honest conversations. This has an impact of hindering the development of mutual understanding and can lead to misunderstandings and unresolved issues.

Controlling Behavior:
Attempts to control or manipulate decisions, actions, or interactions. This may include dictating who one can spend time with or what activities are acceptable. This erodes individual autonomy and can lead to feelings of powerlessness and dependence.

Isolation from Support Systems:
Systematic efforts to isolate an individual from friends, family, or support networks, reduces external perspectives and support, making it easier for manipulative behaviors to thrive.

Lack of Respect for Boundaries:
Disregard for personal boundaries, whether physical, emotional, or digital, undermines trust and can lead to feelings of violation and discomfort.

Constant Criticism:
Regularly belittling, criticizing, or demeaning behavior, damages self-esteem and creates a negative emotional environment.

Unpredictable Mood Swings:
Drastic and unpredictable changes in mood, leading to emotional turbulence. This creates an unstable emotional atmosphere and can contribute to anxiety and stress.

Gaslighting:
Manipulative tactics to make someone doubt their own perceptions, memories, or sanity, undermines self-confidence and may lead to confusion and self-doubt.

Financial Control:
Taking control of finances, restricting access, or using money as a means of manipulation, limits financial independence and can contribute to dependency.

Escalation of Conflict:
A pattern of escalating conflicts, with disagreements turning into intense arguments or physical altercations creates a hostile and unsafe environment.

Lack of Empathy:
Consistent lack of empathy or understanding towards the other person's emotions or experiences, hinders emotional connection and mutual support.

Secrecy and Deception:
Keeping significant aspects of one's life hidden or engaging in deceitful behavior, erodes trust and can lead to feelings of betrayal.

Unhealthy Jealousy:
Excessive jealousy or possessiveness, leading to monitoring and controlling behaviors, strains trust and can contribute to feelings of insecurity.

Dismissal of Concerns:
Dismissing or minimizing concerns raised by the other person. **Impact:** Prevents open communication and resolution of issues.

Pattern of Blame:
Consistent blaming of the other person for problems or challenges, creates a toxic atmosphere and inhibits problem solving.

Physical or Verbal Abuse:
Any form of physical, verbal, or emotional abuse has severe consequences for both mental and physical well-being.

Recognizing these red flags is the first step in addressing potential issues in a relationship. It's essential to trust one's instincts, communicate openly, and seek support if needed. If red flags persist, professional help, such as counseling or therapy, may be beneficial in navigating and resolving relationship challenges.

7.2: Building Resilience and Emotional Intelligence
Building resilience and emotional intelligence are key components for navigating life's challenges, fostering healthy relationships, and promoting personal growth.

Here's a guide on developing these essential skills:

Building Resilience: Develop a Growth Mindset:
Embrace challenges as opportunities for growth. See setbacks as temporary and focus on learning from experiences.

Cultivate Self-awareness:
Understand your strengths, weaknesses, and emotional triggers. Self-awareness is the foundation for building resilience.

Establish Healthy Connections:
Build a supportive network of friends, family, and mentors. Strong social connections provide emotional support during difficult times.

Practice Positive Self Talk:
Challenge negative thoughts with positive and constructive self-talk. Cultivate a mindset that fosters self-encouragement.

Set Realistic Goals:
Break down larger goals into manageable steps. Achieving small milestones boosts confidence and resilience.

Learn from Adversity:
Reflect on past challenges and identify lessons learned. Adversity can be a powerful teacher.

Adopt Healthy Coping Strategies:
Develop healthy coping mechanisms, such as mindfulness, exercise, or creative activities. These strategies contribute to emotional well-being.

Maintain a Sense of Humor:
Find humor in challenging situations. Laughter can be a powerful tool for reducing stress and building resilience.

Adaptability and Flexibility:
Embrace change and uncertainty. Develop adaptability to navigate unexpected challenges with resilience.

Seek Professional Support:
If needed, seek guidance from mental health professionals. Therapists can provide tools and strategies for building emotional resilience.

Developing Emotional Intelligence:
Self-Awareness:
Understand and recognize your own emotions. Regularly check in with yourself to identify how you are feeling.

Self-Regulation:
Develop the ability to manage and regulate your emotions. Practice techniques such as deep breathing or meditation to stay emotionally balanced.

Empathy:
Cultivate empathy by actively listening to others and trying to understand their perspectives and emotions.

Social Skills:
Build effective communication and interpersonal skills. Develop the ability to navigate social situations with empathy and tact.

Motivation:
Set and work towards meaningful goals. Find intrinsic motivation that aligns with your values and aspirations.

Recognize Emotions in Others:
Pay attention to the emotions of those around you. Being attuned to others' feelings enhances social interactions.

Conflict Resolution:
Develop skills in resolving conflicts positively. Approach conflicts with a focus on understanding and finding mutually beneficial solutions.

Cultivate a Positive Outlook:
Choose to see challenges as opportunities. Maintain a positive and optimistic outlook even in the face of difficulties.

Continuous Learning:
Stay open to learning more about emotions and how they impact behavior. Read literature on emotional intelligence and attend relevant workshops.

Practice Mindfulness:
Engage in mindfulness practices to stay present and aware of your emotions. Mindfulness enhances self-awareness and self-regulation.

Feedback and Reflection:
Seek feedback from others about your emotional intelligence. Reflect on how your emotions impact your decisions and relationships.

Balanced Decision Making:
Make decisions with consideration for both emotions and rational thinking. Strive for a balanced approach in decision making.

Cultural Sensitivity:
Understand and appreciate cultural differences in emotional expression. Cultural sensitivity enhances interpersonal relationships.

Teamwork and Collaboration:
Foster a collaborative mindset. Work effectively with others, recognizing and valuing their emotions and contributions.

Resilience as an Aspect of Emotional Intelligence:
Acknowledge that resilience is an integral part of emotional intelligence. Building resilience supports emotional well-being and adaptability.

Integration of Resilience and Emotional Intelligence:
Mind Body Connection:
Recognize the interconnectedness of emotions and physical well-being. Practices that enhance emotional intelligence often contribute to overall resilience.

Reflection and Continuous Improvement:
Regularly reflect on your emotional responses and resilience strategies. Embrace a mindset of continuous improvement in both areas.

Adaptable Mindset:
Develop an adaptable mindset that combines emotional intelligence and resilience to navigate various life circumstances. By intentionally cultivating resilience and emotional intelligence, individuals can navigate life's challenges with greater effectiveness, build meaningful relationships, and contribute to their overall well-being.

7.3: Promoting Healthy Relationship Dynamics:
Healthy relationship dynamics are built on effective communication, mutual respect, and a commitment to understanding and supporting one another. Here's a guide on promoting these essential elements for fostering strong and positive relationships:

Effective Communication:
Active Listening:
Cultivate the habit of active listening. Focus on understanding the speaker's perspective without interrupting or formulating a response prematurely.

Clear and Open Expression:

Express yourself clearly and openly. Use "I" statements to communicate your feelings, needs, and thoughts, fostering a non-confrontational dialogue.

Encourage Dialogue:

Create an environment that encourages open dialogue. Encourage your partner to express their thoughts and emotions without fear of judgment.

Non-Verbal Cues:

Pay attention to nonverbal cues, such as body language and facial expressions. Non-verbal communication provides valuable insights into emotions.

Empathetic Responses:

Respond with empathy to your partner's concerns. Acknowledge their feelings and demonstrate understanding and support.

Use of Positive Language:

Choose positive and constructive language. Avoid negative or accusatory language that may escalate conflicts.

Clarification when Needed:

Seek clarification when aspects of communication are unclear. This helps prevent misunderstandings and ensures alignment.

Regular Check Ins:

Schedule regular check ins to discuss the state of your relationship. Use this time to share feelings, address concerns, and reinforce your connection.

Mutual Respect:

Valuing Individual Autonomy:

Respect each other's autonomy and independence. Allow space for individual growth, personal pursuits, and self-expression.

Equality in Decision Making:

Strive for equality in decision making. Collaborate on choices that impact both partners, ensuring that both voices are heard and valued.

Acknowledgment of Boundaries:
Respect personal boundaries. Understand and acknowledge each other's limits, both physical and emotional, and ensure they are honored.

Appreciation and Gratitude:
Express appreciation and gratitude regularly. Acknowledge each other's contributions, efforts, and positive qualities.

Conflict Resolution with Respect:
Approach conflicts with respect. Focus on the issue at hand rather than resorting to personal attacks. Use "I" statements to express concerns.

Validation of Emotions:
Validate each other's emotions. Acknowledge the validity of your partner's feelings even if you may not fully understand them.

Cultural Sensitivity:
Be culturally sensitive and aware of differences. Respect diverse backgrounds, traditions, and perspectives within the relationship.

Shared Responsibility:
Share responsibilities in the relationship. Establish a sense of partnership by collaboratively managing tasks, chores, and decision making.

Building Trust:
Consistency in Actions:
Be consistent in your actions. Trust is built through reliability and predictability in behavior.

Honesty and Transparency:
Practice honesty and transparency. Open communication and truthfulness contribute to a foundation of trust.

Reliability and Dependability:
Demonstrate reliability and dependability. Follow through on commitments and be someone your partner can count on.

Forgiveness and Second Chances:
Foster a culture of forgiveness. Understand that mistakes happen, and providing second chances contributes to a resilient relationship.

Shared Goals and Values:
Align on shared goals and values. A shared sense of purpose strengthens the foundation of trust and mutual understanding.

Vulnerability and Openness:
Be open and vulnerable with each other. Sharing fears, insecurities, and aspirations builds a deep level of trust and connection.

Respect for Privacy:
Respect each other's privacy. Healthy relationships allow space for individual thoughts, emotions, and personal space. Promoting healthy relationship dynamics requires ongoing effort, effective communication, and a commitment to mutual respect. By fostering an environment of understanding, trust, and open communication, couples can build strong foundations for lasting and fulfilling relationships.

7.4: Early Intervention and Support Systems in Relationships:
Early intervention and support systems play a crucial role in addressing challenges and promoting the well-being of individuals and relationships. Here's a guide on implementing early intervention strategies and establishing robust support systems:

Early Intervention Strategies:
Regular Check Ins:
Schedule regular check ins within the relationship to discuss concerns, feelings, and potential challenges. Early identification of issues allows for proactive resolution.

Open and Honest Communication:
Foster an environment of open and honest communication. Encourage partners to express their thoughts and feelings freely, creating a foundation for early problem solving.

Establishing Boundaries:
Clearly define and respect personal and relationship boundaries. Address any discomfort or violation of boundaries promptly to prevent escalation.

Recognizing Warning Signs:
Educate individuals on recognizing early warning signs of unhealthy dynamics, such as controlling behavior or communication breakdown. Early awareness is key to intervention.

Conflict Resolution Skills:
Equip individuals with effective conflict resolution skills. Provide tools for navigating disagreements constructively and preventing conflicts from escalating.

Accessing Relationship Education:
Encourage participation in relationship education programs. These programs can provide valuable insights into healthy relationship dynamics and communication.

Professional Guidance:
If needed, seek the assistance of relationship counselors or therapists. Professional guidance can address concerns early on and provide strategies for improvement.

Mindfulness and Self Reflection:
Promote mindfulness practices and self-reflection. Encourage individuals to be aware of their thoughts and emotions, facilitating early identification of potential issues.

Establishing Support Systems:
Social Networks:
Cultivate supportive social networks. Encourage individuals to maintain connections with friends and family who can offer emotional support and advice.

Community Resources:
Identify and utilize community resources. Support groups, workshops, and counseling services can provide additional perspectives and assistance.

Peer Support:
Encourage peer support. Having friends or mentors who can offer guidance and share their experiences can be valuable in navigating challenges.

Online Platforms:
Utilize online platforms and forums. Online communities provide a space for individuals to seek advice, share experiences, and access a wealth of information.

Educational Initiatives:
Support educational initiatives that focus on relationship health. Promote awareness and understanding of healthy relationship dynamics.

Mental Health Resources:
Ensure access to mental health resources. Individuals facing challenges should be aware of available resources for professional help and counseling.

Family Support:
Strengthen family support systems. Encourage open communication within families and foster an environment where individuals feel comfortable seeking help.

Employer Support Programs:
Encourage workplace support programs. Employers can play a role in supporting employees through Employee Assistance Programs (EAPs) or counseling services.

Crisis Helplines:
Share information about crisis helplines. Individuals in distress should be aware of available helplines for immediate support.

Educational Campaigns:
Launch educational campaigns on relationship health. Disseminate information about the importance of seeking support early and breaking stigmas around seeking help.

Early Mental Health Screening:
Implement early mental health screening programs. Early identification of mental health concerns contributes to timely intervention and support.

Collaborative Approach:
Interdisciplinary Collaboration:
Foster interdisciplinary collaboration. Professionals from various fields, including mental health, education, and community services, can work together to provide comprehensive support.

Community Engagement:
Engage the community in promoting a culture of support and intervention. Community involvement enhances the availability and accessibility of resources.

Regular Assessments:

Conduct regular assessments of relationship health. Periodic evaluations can identify changes or challenges that require attention.

Continuous Education:

Provide continuous education on relationship well-being. Equip individuals with the knowledge and skills to navigate challenges and seek help when needed.

Research and Development:

Invest in research and development of effective early intervention strategies. Stay informed about evolving methods for addressing relationship issues. Early intervention and robust support systems contribute to the overall health and resilience of individuals and relationships. By creating an environment that encourages open communication, seeks professional guidance when needed, and leverages community resources, we can foster positive and thriving relationships.

Chapter Eight

Recap of Key Concepts

Trauma Bonding: Definition:
Emotional connection formed with an abuser, characterized by a cycle of affection and abuse.

Impact:
Creates emotional dependence, challenges in setting boundaries, and difficulty breaking free from toxic relationships.

Trauma: Definition:
Psychological and emotional response to distressing events that exceed one's coping capacity.

Significance of Trauma Bonding on Mental Health:

Impact:
Emotional dependence, difficulty establishing boundaries, and challenges in forming positive relationships.

Formation of Trauma Bonds:

Neurobiological Aspects:
Involves brain chemistry changes reinforcing the bond.

In Intimate Partner Violence:
Formed through cycles of abuse and apologies.

In Parental Relationships:
May result from inconsistent caregiving and attachment issues.

In Cults and Manipulative Groups:
Exploits vulnerabilities and fosters dependence.

In Friendships and Social Circles:
Can develop through shared traumatic experiences.

Signs and Symptoms of Trauma Bonding:

Emotional Dependence:
Reliance on the abuser for emotional support.

Cyclic Patterns of Abuse and Apology:
Repeating cycles of mistreatment and reconciliation.

Isolation from Supportive Networks:
Limited access to external support.

Breaking the Bonds:
Recognizing and Acknowledging Trauma Bonding:
Self-awareness and acknowledgment of the unhealthy bond.

Therapeutic Approaches:
Cognitive Behavioral Therapy, Dialectical Behavior Therapy, Eye Movement Desensitization and Reprocessing.

Rebuilding and Healing:
Establishing healthy boundaries, accessing support systems.

Preventing Future Bonds:
Education and Awareness:
Recognizing potential red flags in relationships.

Building Supportive Networks:
Cultivating healthy relationships and mutual support.

Promoting Well-being: Emotional and Psychological Well-being:
Focusing on mental health and emotional resilience.

Physical Well-being:
Prioritizing self-care practices and maintaining physical health. These key concepts provide a foundation for understanding, addressing, and preventing trauma bonding. Recognizing the signs, breaking the cycle, and fostering well-being are integral aspects of healing from the impact of trauma bonding.

Encouragement for Recovery and Growth:
Recovering from trauma bonding is a courageous journey towards healing and personal growth. Here's some encouragement along with three success stories that highlight the strength and resilience of individuals who successfully navigated the path to recovery:

Embrace Your Strength:
Recognize the strength within you that allowed you to endure and survive. Your resilience is a powerful force that will guide you through the healing process.

Celebrate Small Wins:
Acknowledge and celebrate each small step forward. Recovery is a series of victories, and every positive change, no matter how small, is a triumph.

Seek Support:
Surround yourself with a supportive network of friends, family, or professionals. Sharing your journey can alleviate the burden and provide valuable insights.

Patience is Key:
Healing is a gradual process, and it's crucial to be patient with yourself. Understand that recovery takes time, and each day brings you closer to a healthier and happier you.

Focus on Self Compassion:
Practice self-compassion. Treat yourself with the same kindness and understanding that you would offer to a friend facing similar challenges.

Set Realistic Goals:
Establish realistic and achievable goals. Breaking down your recovery into manageable steps allows for a sense of accomplishment and progress.

Explore Your Identity:

Take the time to rediscover who you are outside of the trauma. Reconnect with your passions, interests, and values as you rebuild your sense of self.

Cultivate a Supportive Environment:

Create a positive and supportive environment. Surround yourself with people who uplift and inspire you on your journey to recovery.

Chapter Nine

Life After Trauma Bonding

Success Stories:

These stories give heart-warming examples of breaking free from abusive relationships and how they used the strategies in this book to help them rebuild their lives.

Sarah's story:

Meet Sarah, a resilient individual who, despite enduring a trauma-bonded relationship, embarked on a journey of healing and empowerment that transformed her life.

Sarah was entangled in a toxic and emotionally abusive relationship for several years. The trauma bond formed due to cycles of love and manipulation, creating a sense of dependency on her partner. The relationship left Sarah feeling broken, devoid of self-worth, and trapped in a cycle of emotional turmoil.

The turning point came when Sarah recognized the toxicity of the relationship. Despite the emotional pull and fear of separation, she acknowledged the need for change. It was a moment of clarity where Sarah realized that her well-being and sense of self were worth fighting for.

Sarah began therapy with a trauma-informed counselor who specialized in abusive relationships. Through therapy, she explored the dynamics of the trauma bond, understood its impact, and gained tools to break free. Learning to set and maintain healthy boundaries became a crucial aspect of Sarah's journey. She started by clearly defining what behaviors were unacceptable and asserting her right to be treated with respect. Sarah actively sought support from friends, family, and a survivors' support group. Sharing her experiences with empathetic individuals helped diminish feelings of isolation and fostered a sense of community.

Sarah educated herself about the dynamics of trauma bonding, emotional abuse, and the impact on mental health. This knowledge empowered her to recognize unhealthy patterns and provided validation for her experiences.

Engaging in self-care became a priority. Sarah rediscovered activities she once enjoyed, adopted a healthier lifestyle, and practiced mindfulness to reconnect with her inner self.

In Sarah's case, legal intervention was necessary due to the severity of the emotional abuse. She sought a restraining order and took legal steps to protect herself from further harm, reclaiming a sense of control over her life.

Sarah invested time in her education and career. Pursuing new skills and setting professional goals helped her regain a sense of independence and financial stability.

Through therapy, self-reflection, and continuous learning, Sarah embraced personal growth. She worked on overcoming the residual impact of the trauma bond and focused on becoming the person she aspired to be.

Over time, Sarah cautiously opened herself to new relationships, focusing on those built on mutual respect and understanding. She learned to identify and prioritize healthy connections.

Through dedication and resilience, Sarah emerged from the trauma-bonded relationship empowered and transformed. She rebuilt her life, reclaimed her identity, and became an advocate for survivors of emotional abuse.

Sarah's success story illustrates that with the right support, self-care practices, and a commitment to personal growth, it is possible to break free from trauma bonding and build a life filled with empowerment and resilience.

Mia's Story:
Meet Mia, a resilient individual who navigated the challenging path of recovery after being deeply entangled in a cultic environment. Mia's story is a testament to the strength of

the human spirit and the possibility of rebuilding life after escaping the clutches of a manipulative cult.

Mia became involved with a cult during college, attracted by promises of spiritual enlightenment and a sense of belonging. However, the seemingly utopian community soon revealed its darker side, marked by manipulation, control, and exploitation. The experience left Mia emotionally scarred, but a desire for freedom and personal growth became the catalyst for change.

The first step for Mia was recognizing the manipulation tactics employed by the cult. Through therapy and education on coercive control, Mia gained insights into the power dynamics at play. Mia sought the support of a mental health professional experienced in trauma and cult recovery. Therapeutic sessions provided a safe space to process the emotional impact of cult involvement and develop coping strategies.

Establishing connections with other former cult members and participating in support groups played a crucial role. Sharing experiences and insights with individuals who understood the depth of the trauma fostered a sense of community and validation.

Mia actively worked on reclaiming personal autonomy. This involved making decisions independently, rediscovering personal preferences, and learning to trust one's judgment. Education about the psychology of cults and mind control was a pivotal aspect of recovery. Understanding how undue influence operated in the cult allowed Mia to break free from lingering thought patterns.

Mia confronted triggers associated with the cult experience rather than avoiding them. Gradual exposure and desensitization, guided by a therapist, helped reduce the emotional charge associated with traumatic memories. Rebuilding relationships with friends and family outside the cult became a priority. Mia sought reconciliation with loved ones, fostering a sense of belonging beyond the confines of the cult.

Investing time and effort in personal and professional development was instrumental. Pursuing education and career goals provided a sense of purpose and contributed to rebuilding a life outside the cultic environment.

Mia became an advocate for cult awareness, sharing her story to educate others about the dangers of manipulative groups. Engaging in activism provided a sense of purpose and contributed to the healing process. Through resilience, self-discovery, and the support of mental health professionals and a strong community of survivors, Mia successfully broke free from the trauma bonding induced by cult involvement.

Mia's journey is not only a testament to personal strength but also a beacon of hope for others who have faced similar challenges. Today, Mia leads a fulfilling life, dedicated to helping others navigate the path to recovery and resilience after leaving cultic environments.

Louisa's Story
Meet Louisa, a survivor who emerged victorious from the shadows of intimate partner violence (IPV). Louisa's story is a testament to resilience, empowerment, and the transformative journey towards a life free from abuse.

Louisa found herself in an abusive relationship characterized by manipulation, control, and physical violence. As the abuse escalated, Louisa reached a breaking point and made the courageous decision to break free from the cycle of violence.

The first step in Louisa's journey was acknowledging the abuse and understanding that it was not her fault. Education on the dynamics of IPV played a crucial role in recognizing unhealthy patterns. Louisa worked with a domestic violence advocate to create a safety plan. This involved identifying safe spaces, establishing communication strategies, and preparing for potential emergencies.

Louisa engaged with a therapist specializing in trauma and domestic violence. Therapy provided a safe space to process the emotional scars, build coping mechanisms, and develop a path towards healing.

Louisa took legal action to secure a restraining order against her abusive partner. Legal protection became a crucial component of her safety plan, empowering her to reclaim control over her life.

Louisa surrounded herself with a network of friends, family, and support groups. Sharing her experiences with empathetic individuals fostered a sense of community and provided emotional validation. Louisa became an advocate for IPV awareness, sharing her story to educate others about the signs of abuse and the resources available for survivors. Her advocacy work aimed to break the silence surrounding domestic violence.

Achieving financial independence was a significant milestone for Louisa. With the support of community resources and employment assistance, she gained control over her finances, reducing vulnerability to further manipulation. Therapy and support groups played a vital role in rebuilding Louisa's self-esteem. Affirmative practices, self-love exercises, and positive affirmations contributed to a more positive self-perception. Louisa learned to establish and maintain healthy boundaries in relationships. Through therapy, she explored healthy communication patterns, fostering connections based on mutual respect and understanding. Louisa rekindled her aspirations by pursuing educational and career goals. With the support of mentors and career guidance, she found a renewed sense of purpose and self-worth.

Louisa's transformative journey led to a life free from the shackles of intimate partner violence. She not only broke the cycle of abuse but also became an advocate, inspiring others to seek help and fostering awareness about the impact of domestic violence.

Today, Louisa thrives as a symbol of resilience, empowerment, and transformation. Her story exemplifies the strength that survivors possess and the possibility of rebuilding a life filled with safety, self-love, and hope after intimate partner violence. Louisa's journey is a beacon for those still trapped in the darkness of abuse, showing that there is a way out and a path towards a brighter future. These success stories illustrate that recovery is possible.

With courage, support, and the commitment to personal growth, individuals can emerge from trauma bonding stronger, wiser, and ready to embrace a healthier and more fulfilling life. Your journey is unique, and every step forward is a triumph in itself.

Chapter Ten

More Information on Trauma Bonding

Expert insights on trauma bonding, recovery, and fostering healthy relationships:

Trauma Bonding:

Dr. Judith Herman, Psychiatrist and Trauma Expert: "Trauma bonding often stems from a survival instinct in the face of abusive situations. Understanding the neurobiological aspects is crucial for both individuals and professionals working in the field of trauma."

Dr. Bessel van der Kolk, Trauma Researcher and Author: "Trauma bonds can be tenacious, but breaking free is possible through interventions that address the body, mind, and emotions. Integrative therapies, such as EMDR and somatic experiencing, can be instrumental in the recovery process."

Recovery:

Dr. Christine Courtois, Clinical Psychologist and Trauma Specialist: "Recovery from trauma bonding involves not just breaking the bond but also rebuilding a sense of self. It requires a comprehensive approach, including therapy, support systems, and self-compassion."

Dr. Peter Levine, Somatic Experiencing Founder: "The body holds the key to healing from trauma. Somatic practices that address the physical manifestations of trauma can complement traditional therapeutic approaches and support a more holistic recovery."

Fostering Healthy Relationships:

Dr. John Gottman, Relationship Researcher: "Building and maintaining a healthy relationship involves continuous positive interactions. the 'magic ratio' of positive to negative interactions is a key factor in predicting the success of a relationship."

Dr. Sue Johnson, Founder of Emotionally Focused Therapy: "Emotional connection is at the core of healthy relationships. Recognizing and responding to each other's emotional needs fosters a sense of security and intimacy."

Self-care and Well-being:

Dr. Nadine Burke Harris, Surgeon General of California: "Recognizing the impact of trauma on overall health is essential. Prioritizing self-care practices, including mindfulness and exercise, can mitigate the long-term effects of trauma."

Dr. Kristin Neff, Self-Compassion Researcher: "Self-compassion is a powerful tool in the recovery journey. Treating yourself with kindness and understanding, especially during challenging times, enhances resilience and well-being."*

Early Intervention and Support:

Dr. Mary P. Koss, Clinical Psychologist and Advocate: "Early intervention is crucial in addressing the pervasive impact of trauma. Encouraging survivors to seek support, whether through friends, family, or professionals, can interrupt the cycle of abuse."

Dr. Bruce Perry, Child Psychiatrist and Neuroscientist: "Children are particularly vulnerable to the effects of trauma. Early intervention programs that focus on building a child's resilience and providing a safe environment can prevent long term negative outcomes."

These insights from experts highlight the multidimensional nature of trauma, recovery, and the importance of healthy relationships. Integrating various therapeutic approaches, fostering emotional connections, and promoting early intervention are key components in supporting individuals on their journey to healing and well-being.

Suggested reading

Carnes, P. (1998). The Betrayal Bond: Breaking Free of Exploitive Relationships. Health Communications. This book delves into the psychology of betrayal bonds, providing insights into why individuals stay in harmful relationships and offering strategies for breaking free.

Thomas, S. (2016). Healing from Hidden Abuse: A Journey Through the Stages of Recovery from Psychological Abuse. MAST Publishing House. Focusing on emotional and psychological abuse, Thomas guides readers through the process of recognizing and healing from hidden abuse, including trauma bonding.

Evans, P. (2018). The Verbally Abusive Relationship: How to Recognize It and How to Respond. Adams Media. Evans explores verbal abuse in relationships and the psychological effects it can have, including the formation of trauma bonds. The book provides guidance on recognizing and responding to abuse.

Journal Articles:

Dorey, Kathysue. (2022). A Traumatology Focus on Trauma Bonding. https://www.researchgate.net/publication/ 364294067_A_Traumatology_Focus_on_ Trauma_Bonding

Miranda Olff (2012) Bonding after trauma: on the role of social support and the oxytocin system in traumatic stress, European Journal of Psychotraumatology, 3:1, DOI: 10.3402/ejpt. v3i0.18597

Ronald Chambers, Matthew Gibson, Sarah Chaffin, Timothy Takag i, Nancy Nguyen & Toussaint Mears Clark (2022) Trauma coerced Attachment and Complex PTSD: Informed Care for Survivors of Human Trafficking, Journal of Human Trafficking, DOI: 10.1080/23322705.2021.2012386

About the Author

Harper Emerson is a passionate and empathetic writer who delves into the complex and often misunderstood world of trauma bonding. With no formal qualifications, Harper relies on her keen observational skills and personal experiences to explore the intricate dynamics of relationships shaped by trauma. Drawing inspiration from her own journey and the stories of those around her, Harper courageously navigates the uncharted territories of emotional entanglements, offering readers a raw and unfiltered perspective on the subject.

Harper's unique approach to writing stems from her genuine curiosity about the human condition and her desire to shed light on the silent struggles many face in their relationships. Her work is a testament to the power of personal narratives and the strength that can be found in vulnerability. Although she may not hold traditional qualifications, Harper's authenticity, and sincerity shine through in her writing, creating a space for readers to reflect on their own experiences and find solace in the shared aspects of the human experience.

In this book, Harper Emerson invites readers to embark on a journey of self-discovery and healing, encouraging them to break free from the chains of unhealthy relationships. Through her words, she aims to empower individuals to recognize the signs of trauma bonding, embrace their own resilience, and ultimately foster healthier connections with themselves and others.

Also By

Other books written by Harper Emerson

Printed in Great Britain
by Amazon